CULTURAL & ECONOMIC
REVITALIZATION

CULTURAL & ECONOMIC REVITALIZATION

A Five-Step Reference
for Overcoming Black Failure

NIQUE FAJORS

ISBN: 0-9666734-0-9
Library of Congress Catalog Card Number: 98-75016

Cover Photograph by Ray Grist
Cover design by Angie Johnson Art Productions
Layout and Design by Dageforde Publishing, Inc.

CULTURAL & ECONOMIC REVITALIZATION
Nique Fajors
P.O. Box 118148
Chicago, IL 60611-8148

Printed in the United States of America

10 9 8 7 6 5 4 3 2 1

DEDICATION

This book is dedicated to every woman, man, and child of African ancestry who has suffered under the chains of exploitation, oppression, and rape for the past 600 years. I would not exist without your courage, bravery, and commitment to your own humanity.

CONTENTS

ACKNOWLEDGMENTS

*T*hanks to Rhonda Redd for editorial direction and thanks to Ray Grist, Demetrios Coupounas, Professor Warren Briggs, Professor James Heskett, Christine Fajors, Herb Fajors, Adrian Hyde, Bronwyn Morgan, Ian Rowe, McLean Mashingaidze Greaves, Seymour George Hall, Nananamibia Smith, Kabari Jordan, Althea Green, Bennie Smith, Ariel Rosen, Adrienne Kent, Dageforde Publishing, Inc., and several other people who gave their valuable time to help me complete this book.

Proceeds of ten percent of net book sales will be contributed to the Washington Interdependence Council's initiative to erect a monument in Washington, DC to Mr. Benjamin Banneker (1731-1806), American's first Black Man of Science.

PREFACE

A wareness is the first step to change. I have written this book to raise the awareness of the relevant issues that affect people of African ancestry. Most of what I present is not new. In the presentation and structure, I hope to reach more people who might not have otherwise thought about the issues within the context that I frame them.

My goal is to cause you to engage deeply in the issues and problems that face people of African ancestry. As we enter the 21st Century, we have two paths that we can follow. One will lead toward renewed excellence and revitalization; the other path will lead to cultural and mental extinction.

My Cultural and Economic Revitalization (CER) model is created out of the brilliant works of the late Dr. Cheikh Anta Diop. Dr. Diop was one of the great minds of the 20th Century. He was born in Diourbel, Senegal on December 29, 1923. At age 23, he went to Paris to continue advanced studies in physics. Within a very short time, however, he was drawn deeper and deeper into studies of the origin of civilization in Africa. Becoming increasingly active in the African student movements agitating for independence of French colonial possessions, he became convinced that only by re-evaluating and restoring Africa's place in the history of the world could the physical and mental shackles of colonialism be lifted from Africa.

Dr. Diop was Director of the Radiocarbon Laboratory at the Fundamental Institute of Black Africa (IFAN) at the University of Dakar. He sat on numerous international scientific committees and achieved recognition as one of the leading historians, Egyptologists, linguists, and anthropologists in the world. He was the pharaoh of African studies. He died in his sleep in Dakar on February 7, 1986.[1]

Dr. Diop's work on ancient African cultures and philosophies represents much of what we search for from other cultures and philosophies today — answers to our problems. How sad it is that we search the culture of our historic oppressors for answers to the problems that they helped create for us.

This book is grounded in the reality of failure that African people have seen and felt for the last 600 years. Imperialists (European and Arab) understood they had to kill us culturally before trying to physically overwhelm us. The problem of black people throughout the world today is fundamentally a cultural one. We, as a people, have adopted the cultural values of every people but ourselves. We are culturally inconsistent. This inconsistency does not provide us with a shared valued system to build and maintain vibrant and loving communities.

Thus, step one on the path to cultural and economic revitalization is to become a culturally consistent individual. This process begins with a reorientation back to a matriarchal view of society, similar to many successful, ancient African civilizations. To be culturally consistent requires you to know your history, to practice a spirituality that celebrates the African in you, and to remove from your vocabulary the words of oppression. This must be step one in your program for revitalization.

Step two in the process begins by creating an environment of love around you. First, you create it within yourself, then within your family, and finally your entire community is enveloped in your environment of love. Within the family context, the focus is on relationships, partner selection, and raising a family. Once African people begin to respect and love themselves (achieved by becoming culturally consistent), that attitude and behavior will be passed on and shared in our friendships and our communities. The result will be an environment that celebrates humanity and supports excellence.

Step three is educational excellence. This is an area where many movements begin their efforts. The step begins with vision. Our children imitate what they see. If we expose our children to negative images and dysfunctional role models, they will grow into those images. The home is a far more important place of learning than school. Unfortunately, at

1   Ivan Van Sertima, *Great African Thinkers*, Cheikh Anta Diop (New Jersey: Transaction Books), p. 8-10.

home too many parents abandon their children to television. Television can cripple a child's self worth. The library must be one of your child's best friends. Within the context of educational excellence, it is the parents' responsibility to ensure that their children are receiving an education that celebrates their ancestral brilliance every day, not just one month out of the year.

Community empowerment is step four. To affect real change in this area requires a change in perspective. We must begin to view ourselves as the customers of our local, state, and federal government. We pay them to provide us the services we require. We pay for the police force. We pay for garbage collection. We must begin to create real accountability in our politicians. Too many of our black politicians get a free ride just because they are black and belong to the Democratic party. They run into an ethical problem and they claim the racist system is targeting them—sometimes it is, but sometimes they are merely parasites making a wonderful career out of our collective misery. No group in our communities receives as little deserved criticism as our politicians.

Many efforts at improving our communities have failed, not because of lack of effort or even resources, but because they were not integrated into a larger context. We all agree that economic development is critical to the sustainability and growth of our communities, but I maintain that it must be the last step in a five step process.

Black, white, and Asian groups that have traveled to America and achieved economic success have one element that most African Americans do not have—a common, shared cultural foundation that did not develop out of a holocaust [African slavery]. African Americans have built a culture out of cultural oppression. To make us better slaves, our culture was ripped from us. To create sustainable economic development, we must have trust, integrity, understanding, and respect in our communities. Culture is the basket each of these critical elements can gather. Can you imagine if Jewish people decided to center their culture around their 20th Century holocaust versus their more than 3,000 year old culture? Their economic success is largely a function of their ability to maintain their empowering ancient culture.

To note, each step has three phases that are detailed in each chapter. By embracing the CER model, I believe people of African ancestry can achieve lasting success. The end result of cultural and economic revitalization is economically strong, loving, and supportive African-centered families. The phases of the results are presented below:

Result 1. Teenage Pregnancy (down)
Result 2. Drug Use (down)
Result 3. Violent Crimes (down)
Result 4. Blacks in Prison (down)
Result 5. Two Parent Homes (up)
Result 6. Infant Mortality (down)
Result 7. Life Expectancy (up)
Result 8. Black Graduates from College (up)
Result 9. Black Businesses (up)
Result 10. Ownership of Our Creativity (Sports and Entertainment)
Result 11. City Dominance (New York, Atlanta, Chicago, and Washington D.C.)
Result 12. Cultural Bridges with Africans (Americas, Polynesia, Australia, Asia, and Africa)
Result 13. Economic Bridges with Africans
Result 14. Global Independence and Respect

Black Woman

Black woman you are so special to me.
Out of the mud you raised the whole planet with love, respect, and passion.
You created our capacity to learn, to reproduce.
With your black mate you created, loved, and protected the family.
From the family every nation on this planet has risen.
Every disciple, demi-god, priest, pope, minister, messenger, monk, bishop, saint,
and spirit was born from you.
You are the only true God.

Your beauty is unmatched.
Your body is a temple where only the holiest may pray.
Brown is the color I see when I dream of perfection.
Have I disrespected you in the past?
Forgive my ignorance, my pettiness, I am still but a child.
Like a child I admire, envy, and love you all at the same time.

Why am I so blessed to see you, to know you, to talk to you,
to touch you, to love you?
I know why.
It is because I came from you.

STEP ONE
Cultural Consistency

And They Took

They took the African and said you are now a Negro
And they took the Negro and said you are now inferior to me
And they took this inferior person and said you are now a Christian and the
Negro said, "thank you Father"
And they took the Christian and said you will now treat your wife as a second
class citizen and the Negro said, "all praises to Allah"
And they took this simple minded, God fearing, Sexist and called him
American and the Negro said, "thanks Boss"

During the summer of 1964, El-hajj Malik El-Shabazz (Malcolm X) described the evolution of racism: "... it was only after the spirit of the Black man [and woman] was completely broken and his desire to be a man was completely destroyed, that they [Europeans] took the physical chains from his ankles and put them on his mind." A goal of this book is to help you first see your mental chains and then take action to remove those chains of racism. The first phase in that process is to learn about your culture–your African culture.

I use the Diopian definition of culture. *Culture is central to the development of the national consciousness, which in turn is the mainstay in building and maintaining a civilization.*[2] It is your history, your spirituality, and your language.

In January 1965, El-hajj Malik El-Shabazz captured in another speech the fundamental problem for African people throughout the world.

---

2   Cheikh Anta Diop, *The Cultural Unity of Black Africa* (Chicago: Third World Press), p. 225.

Negro [or Black] doesn't tell you anything....What do you identify it with? Tell me. Nothing.... It doesn't give you a language, because there is no such thing as a Negro language. It doesn't give you a country, because there is no such thing as a Negro country. It doesn't give you a culture—there is no such thing as a Negro culture—it doesn't exist. And this is the position that you and I are in here in America. Formerly, we could be identified by the names we wore when we came here.... But once our names were taken and our language was taken and our identity was destroyed and our roots were cut off with no history, we became like a stump, something dead.

The term Negro can be replaced with Black or Haitian or African American or Brazilian. None of these labels represent a culture that is African. They represent African culture beaten and raped by European exploitation. We cannot build a civilization, or even a community, based on despair, confusion, and self hatred. The direction and many answers lie in some of the culture(s) of ancient Africa.

Jewish people can live in any country on earth and, in most instances, they share common values with other Jewish people. An African from St. Louis, San Juan, and San Paulo share very little. Each African has a unique "culture" that was created during the enslavement of their ancestors by different groups. The few things they do share—musical rhythms, food preparation, and dance—represent the strands of African culture that we were able to maintain from our original home.

History

Phase one in the process of becoming culturally consistent is knowing the history of your ancestors. The foundation of African civilization is the Nile Valley civilizations, Kemite, Nubia, and Ethiopia. For us, the return to the Nile Valley civilizations in every domain is the necessary condition to reconcile African civilization with history. The Nile Valley plays the same role in the rethinking and renewing of African culture that ancient Greece and Rome play in the culture of the Western Europe.

By successive migrations as time passed, Africans slowly penetrated the heart of the continent, spreading out in all directions and dislodging the Pygmies. They founded states that developed and main- tained relations with the mother valley until it was stifled by foreigners. From south to north, these were Nubia and Egypt; from north to south, Nubia and Zimbabwe; from east to west, Nubia, Ghana, Ife; from east to southwest, Nubia, Chad, the Congo; from west to east, Nubia and Ethiopia.[3]

In Zimbabwe stands an array of ruins including a complex of buildings consisting of walls, towers, rounded gateways, and steps. The two most prominent buildings have been identified as the acropolis and the temple. All are made of local granite that is flat and brick-like. All of these structures were built without any mortar or cement. The ruins and monuments are found over a radius of 100 miles around Victoria.[4]

Civilizations created by people of African ancestry were not just based in Africa. The ancient Dravidian civilizations of India were an outgrowth of people from the Nile Valley. The indigenous people of Australia, who today call themselves Black Australians, created amazing art work of their dreamtime world tens of thousands of years ago.

There have been several people in our recent history who understood the importance of ancient Africa in the lives of modern Africans. One of these prophets is Dr. Diop, another is The Honorable Marcus Mosiah Garvey.

As I learn more about Marcus Garvey, I am overwhelmed by his courage and vision. And I am deeply saddened by how some of us contributed directly to his imprisonment, deportation, and death.

> *Rather than looking for the pie in the sky,*
> *let's plant the potato.*
> —Marcus Garvey

His first publication, *Negro World* was published in English, Spanish, and French. It was a global newspaper. It was banned in most of Africa and the Caribbean by Europeans. The Europeans were concerned that the potential readers would no longer be satisfied with being European subjects.

> *The NAACP stands for the national association*
> *for the advancement of certain people.*
> (A belief shared by the great Ida B. Wells)
> —Marcus Garvey

---

3   Cheikh Anta Diop, *The African Origin of Civilization, Myth or Reality* (Chicago: Lawrence Hill Books, 1974), p. 156.

4   Cheikh Anta Diop, *The African Origin of Civilization, Myth or Reality* (Chicago: Lawrence Hill Books, 1974), p. 157.

STEP ONE

One of his U.S.A.-based businesses created the first mass produced black doll for our children. His organization created the red, black, and green flag. He also created the African Orthodox Church, which worships a black Jesus and a black Madonna. From the very beginning of Mr. Garvey's work, women took leadership positions throughout his organizations. In fact, as early as 1914, six women were on the Board of Management for the Universal Negro Improvement Association (UNIA).

Be Black, Buy Black, Think Black.
—Marcus Garvey

The Honorable Mr. Garvey was transforming people right out of slavery. He began his work about ten years after Brazil legally ended the enslavement of human beings. This was not the revolutionary 1960s. There was no television or radio. Yet, Mr. Garvey built a movement with over six million dedicated members. Mr. Garvey's leadership, moral philosophy, cultural understanding, and business acumen touched every ethical, results-oriented leader of African ancestry who followed him. As we enter the 21st Century, we would be wise to immerse ourselves in Mr. Garvey's teachings.

While there are many leaders that have risen to greatness due to their incredible intellect and bravery, others have been selected by groups outside of our community. Which one of our "leaders" stated the following throughout the late 19th Century and early 20th Century?

"If in the providence of God the Negro got any good out of slavery, he got the habit of work."[5]

"We went into slavery without a language; we came out speaking the proud Anglo-Saxon tongue."[6]

The answer is Booker T. Washington. He told white men what they wanted to hear and he got most of their guilt money. He took that money and created several useful institutions. He also used that money and power to destroy other black people who did not want to follow his direction. To note, his most famous book, *Up From Slavery* was ghostwritten by Max Bennett, a white Vermont newspaperman.[7]

---

5   David Levering Lewis, *W.E.B. DuBois Biography of a Race* (New York: Henry Holt and Company), p. 169.
6   Lewis, p. 169.
7   Lewis, p. 262.

5

Booker T. Washington believed that slavery gave us good work habits and we got to learn a new language. In examining slavery in the Americas, I do not see the creation of work habits. I see an undying commitment to be a free people.

The history of black women and men who fought white imperialism and racism during the 18th and 19th Century is a proud record. The Maroons of Suriname beat the Dutch into submission, freeing themselves from slavery. Today, the Maroons remain an intact culture and society in Suriname. The Maroons of Jamaica are famous for keeping the British army at bay for hundreds of years. They remain an important part of Jamaican culture.

The Haitian Revolution from 1791 to 1804 was the most successful slave revolution in history. They fought their way out of bondage and captured complete state power. To note, the Haitian freedom fighters not only beat the French, but they also beat the Spanish and the British. In fact, they invaded the area of their island now called the Dominican Republic and took it from the Spanish, gaining complete control of Hispaniola. For a time, the United States of America feared that Haiti would invade the southern U.S. and free their brothers and sisters from bondage.

One of the main reasons for the success of the Haitians was that most of them were directly from Africa. Slavery on the Island of Hispaniola was so harsh that the average life expectancy of an enslaved person was six years. Thus, new Africans were needed on a regular basis. Native Africans still had an indigenous culture and a historic identity. They knew who the enemy was and fought with great passion. For many years during and after the revolution, Haitians plotted to take an army to West Africa and destroy slavery at the root. They never achieved this goal, but Haiti remains the home of some of the greatest freedom fighters in the history of the world.[8]

Revolution was also the order of the day during the 1960s and 1970s. People were working to overturn practices and behaviors that were as old as America itself. The power structure took action and systematically killed, deported, or paid off almost every leader of any relevant movement. Those who were paid off became contributors to the selfishness that was the 1980s.

---

8 The historic facts presented on Haiti were taken from a lecture by Professor Tony Martin on 3/1/97 in Harlem, NY U.S.A.

STEP ONE

In the early 1960s, many newly independent African nations had stronger economies than many of their Asian counterparts. What happened? Some African nations were left with stronger economies, but they were culturally crippled. While Asian nations were left with little material infrastructure by their colonizers, they maintained their historic language, they continued to worship a God(s) that looked like them, and they retained a firm grasp of their history. The newly freed African nations now spoke the language of their historic oppressors and worshiped a God that looked like their historic oppressors. Many worked to become better Europeans versus better Africans. The results are clear. In the late 1990s, though most of Asia is suffering through a severe economic downturn, it has its sovereignty and is respected. Africa is largely owned and controlled by French, Lebanese, Dutch, English, and Indians and is not respected.

During the early 1970s, the Democratic Republic of the Congo, formerly Zaire, was touted as having the potential to be a developed nation in twenty years. It was to be an example of African excellence. Today, the country is completely destroyed. In 1997, its citizens gave their lives to remove a black dictator, worse than the Europeans who ruled the country before him. Greed, excessive ego, stupidity, self hatred, and selfishness contributed greatly to these 20th Century failures.

Thankfully, there are several organizations and leaders in Africa that understand the importance of their cultures and are working to create nation-building institutions. Mr. Sabelo Sibanda, based in Zimbabwe's second largest city of Bulawayo, has established the School of African Awareness (SAA). Launched on Africa Day, May 25, 1997, the organization's primary thrust is to address issues pertaining to cultural awareness and self-reliance.

"The school was established as a response to the needs of global African people," Sibanda said in a 1998 interview with the Pan African News Agency. "It will try to re-focus the African mentality, to revive our pride and self-esteem so that we can know exactly who we are. The school will try to re-shape our identity by raising a global African consciousness."

Having worked extensively with and among African communities overseas, he came to appreciate what African people could achieve for themselves. Propelled by the work of visionaries such as Marcus Garvey and Malcolm X who made tireless efforts to empower African people from the grassroots level, Sibanda returned home to establish a "school of thought" which aspires to enhance African development and progress.[9]

Addressing the second Southern African International Dialogue in 1998, South Africa's deputy president, Thabo Mbeki, called on African governments to draw up common programs that will address the challenges of the continent. He stated that we have to build a culture to share experience as well as knowledge.

He added that this can only be attained through a united offensive by all the people of Africa, and further asking, "How do we do it and are we willing to do it?" Mbeki who spoke widely on the African Renaissance, said that it was disappointing most Africans do not know about each other's cultures, but were only "experts on American cultural products and know nothing about their arts."[10]

An investigation and discussion of history and culture is most relevant when it provides a nation, community, or family with a value system. In examining some of the most successful ancient African civilizations, matriarchy provided the value system.

One of our greatest kingdoms was Nubia. Women played a leadership role in that society. During the golden age of the Meroitic period, ten different queens ruled. Additionally, six other queens who ruled with their husbands were considered very significant. Many of these rulers were immortalized in statuary. In one instance, a queen was immortalized killing her enemies. In the ancient world, this type of representation did not exist outside of Africa. The queens of Nubia were often portrayed as full-figured. They were called both *gore*, meaning ruler, and *kandake*, meaning queen mother. Kandake has been translated into the English form "Candace."

Dr. Diop informs us that during the entire history of the Egypt of the Pharaohs, African women enjoyed complete freedom, as opposed to the condition of the segregated Indo-European woman of the classical periods, whether she was Greek or Roman. He further informs us that "no evidence can be found either in literature or in historical records relating to the systematic ill-treatment of Egyptian women by their men." They were respected and went about freely and unveiled, unlike certain Asian women. Affection for one's mother and especially the respect

---

9   Memory Mzilethi, *Dream Of A Culturally-Rich Africa*, PanAfrican News Agency , 10 July 1998.
10   Naidoo, Mbeki *On African Renaissance*, PanAfrican News Agency , 28 July 1998.

with which it was necessary to surround her were the most sacred of duties.[11]

Ethiopia was the first country in the world to have been ruled by a queen. Some of the greatest female rulers of the ancient world came from the Nile Valley. One of their greatest achievements was their partnership with men in building lasting states and societies. The African woman, even after marriage, retained all her individuality and her legal rights; she continued to bear the name of her family, in contrast to the Indo-European woman who lost hers to take on that of her husband.[12]

As late as the turn of the century, the Mende of Liberia also practiced equality in the governance of their society. The great Madam Yoko governed fourteen separate chiefdoms in the course of her reign.[13] Within that context, women maintained their own spiritual and cultural associations. The Sande was a secret society for women only, and the Bundu Masks were worn only by women during particular festivals.

This is the one ancient cultural theme that we must return to as a people. *Nothing comes before respect for women.* Scholars can argue for years as to which African cultures, if any, provide a model for modern Africans. What cannot be argued is the need for us to return to a matriarchical model for the betterment of our communities. Equality is not a modern feminist construct. It is a spiritually based African life philosophy. Matriarchy is not an absolute and cynical triumph of woman over man; it is a harmonious dualism, an association accepted by both sexes, the better to build a sedentary society where each and everyone could fully develop by following the activity best suited to his physiological nature. A matriarchal regime, far from being imposed on man by circumstances independent of his will, is accepted and defended by him.[14]

Islam had a shattering effect on the matriarchy in Africa.[15] Over several centuries, it transformed several West African nations from matriarchal to dysfunctional patriarchal societies. In fact, invaders, whether they were Arabs or Europeans, practiced a war on our African customs, religion, and values. In most cases, the first custom they attacked was the matriarchy. They attacked our greatest strength—love and respect for the

---

11 Cheikh Anta Diop, *The Cultural Unity of Black Africa* (Chicago: Third World Press), p. 62.

12 Diop, p. 49.

13 DuSable Museum of African American History, Chicago, IL, Mande/Amistad Exhibit July, 1998.

14 Diop, p. 120.

15 Diop, p. xiii.

African woman. Over time, Africans who had been converted to Islam embraced the patriarchal model of society—male dominance over females. It is the same with the Africans who adopted (or were forced to adopt) Christianity.

Ancient Germanic society offers some insights into the patriarchal model. "The father of the family had extensive rights over his wife whom he could expel if she were unfaithful, whom he could even sell in case of necessity, and over his children whom he could abandon...."[16] The abandonment of children and the burial of infant girls, considered useless mouths to feed, were common practices throughout the whole of the patriarchal Eurasian world.[17] The chart presented below distinguishes between matrilineal and patrilineal characterisitcs. It is taken from Dr. Diop's final book, *Civilization or Barbarism*.

Matrilineal	Patrilineal
Sedentary	Nomadic
Subsistence based on agriculture	Subsistence based on raising cattle
Burial of the dead	Cremation of the dead
Wife may divorce her husband	Wife is property of the husband
Land is an indivisible collective property	Land is private property
The sense of community is highly developed	Individualism is the supreme virtue
No notion of original sin	Notion of original sin
Evil is introduced by men: Seth murders Osiris	Evil is introduced by women: Eve eats the apple
Pacifistic morality	Warrior morality

It is important to note that our decline as a people occurred as we moved from the left column to the right. It will require your personal initiative and commitment to return to many of the timeless virtues of the left column.

---

16 Cheikh Anta Diop, *The Cultural Unity of Black Africa* (Chicago: Third World Press), p. 131.
17 Diop, p. 132.

Spirituality

Phase two in the process of becoming culturally consistent is worshiping a God that looks like you and reflects your cultural foundation. As Dr. Maulana Karenga points out, the quest for spiritual enrichment among black people in the physical and cultural Diaspora has led to the adoption of the Holy Books of other people: the Torah, the Bible and the Quran. Ironically, the sacred literature of ancient Egypt, which predates those texts by thousands of years, is the source of much of the wisdom in those Holy Books. The fact that black people could find spiritual comfort in those alien scriptures speaks both to the African contributions to those religions and the intensity of the African spiritual quest. With all due regard to the black tradition within the so-called great religions, it is now time to "return to the source."[18]

This is an area where I see the greatest resistance to change. In particular, the older you are the less likely you will be willing to explore new spiritual paths. Once an enslaved person reached forty years of age, the slave master rested a little easier. He knew that forty years of cultural oppression and brain washing would most often produce a good, loyal slave. My principles on this matter are clear. I will not practice any religion that requires me to turn my attention away from Africa as the cradle of spirituality (i.e., looking to Mecca or Jerusalem), presents women as second to men, or asks me to worship an image that looks nothing like my ancestors.

The largest Roman Catholic church in the world outside of the Vatican is in the Ivory Coast (a country located on the west coast of Africa). There are no African images in this church. Do you think it likely that non-African people would build a church of any size to worship African deities? The church has twenty-four-hour air conditioning, yet, just a few miles away, some people do not have running water or sewage systems. This is the same country that was in the news in 1998 for reports of slavery. It was uncovered that farmers in the Ivory Coast were enslaving boys from neighboring Mali to work in their fields.

An examination of African adoption of foreign religions is complex. In some instances, beaten in war by superior technology, Africans accepted the invaders as stronger and adopted their religion. In

---

18 Maulana Karenga, Selections from *The Husia* (Los Angeles: The University of Sankore Press, 1984), p. ix.

other instances, we freely adopted foreign spiritual practices. Several great Islamic-centered empires existed during the Middle Ages in West Africa.

Often times the invader used flaws in our existing spiritual system to try to convince us to abandon it. To my surprise, this was often successful in West Africa. In Nigeria, for example, some Nigerians, instead of modernizing aspects of their existing (and ancient) spiritual system (as the Europeans had done with their own system), literally threw the baby out with the bath water and became devout Christians.

One of my greatest frustrations with so-called modern religions is the sexism that exists in them. Biblical scholars agree that the Bible does not accurately portray the role of women who were followers of Jesus Christ during the first century. Take the Virgin Mary, for example. There may be more images of the mother of Jesus Christ than of any other woman in the world. Yet, religious scholars say she is barely mentioned in the Bible after the first Christmas.

During the 1st Century, scholars estimate there were as many women disciples of Jesus as there were men. Like the men, the women were drawn from the villages along the Sea of Galilee. But the men who compiled the scriptures chose to downplay the role of women.

Many scholars believe the role of women was downplayed in an effort to make Christianity more appealing to the pagan Greek and Roman patriarchal societies. Paintings of Jesus at the last supper show him surrounded by men. But scholars say those are prime examples of the distortion of history. Religious scholars say women helped financially support the work of Christ and his apostles, and that women paid for some of the earliest Christian churches.

Many Africans throughout the world have adopted the ten commandments as their life principles. I urge you to return to the source of the ten commandments and adopt the forty-two Declarations of Innocence that were written by Africans more than 3,000 years before the ten commandments were drafted from the forty-two (see below).

1. I have not done iniquity.
2. I have not robbed with violence.
3. I have not stolen.
4. I have done no murder; I have done no harm.
5. I have not defrauded offerings.
6. I have not diminished obligations.

7. I have not plundered the Netcher.[19]
8. I have not spoken lies.
9. I have not snatched away food.
10. I have not caused pain.
11. I have not committed fornication.
12. I have not caused shedding of tears.
13. I have not dealt deceitfully.
14. I have not transgressed.
15. I have not acted guilefully.
16. I have not laid waste the ploughed land.
17. I have not been an eavesdropper.
18. I have not set my lips in motion.
19. I have not been angry and wrathful except for a just cause.
20. I have not defiled the wife of any man.
21. I have not defiled the wife of any man [it was repeated].
22. I have not polluted myself.
23. I have not caused terror.
24. I have not transgressed [repeat twice].
25. I have not burned with rage.
26. I have not stopped my ears against the words of Right and Truth (Maat[20]).
27. I have not worked grief.
28. I have not acted with insolence.
29. I have not stirred up strife.
30. I have not judged hastily.
31. I have not been an eavesdropper [repeated twice].
32. I have not multiplied words exceedingly.
33. I have not done neither harm nor ill.
34. I have never cursed the king.
35. I have never fouled the water.
36. I have not spoken scornfully.
37. I have never cursed the Netcher (a manifestation of God).
38. I have not stolen.
39. I have not defrauded the offerings of the Netcher.
40. I have not plundered the offerings to the blessed dead.
41. I have not filched the food of the infant, neither have I sinned against the Netcher of my native town.
42. I have not slaughtered with evil intent the cattle of the Netcher.

---

19 The personification of one of the divine principles of the Creator.

20 Maat is associated with the seven cardinal virtues, the keys to human perfectibility: truth, justice, propriety, harmony, balance, reciprocity and order.

Language

The real basis of culture is language.[21] How can we hope to work towards a rebirth while speaking exclusively the language of our historic oppressors. Phase three in the process of becoming culturally consistent is integrating your historical languages into the slave-based languages of Europe. You are not expected to learn a new language, but language integration is critical. The language integration should focus on words of love, family, and friendship. Importantly, we must recognize that wherever we live, we should be fluent speakers of the native language. Until our schools in America are able to produce children that have mastered the English language, we should not spend precious resources teaching a pseudo, hybrid language (Ebonics) that grew out of our enslavement.

As you integrate culturally relevant words into your vocabulary, you must remove the oppressive words that the slave master forced upon our ancestors. One of the clearest examples that many African Americans are suffering from a great mental illness is the increasing use of the word nigger. I do not understand why we get such great joy out of using the word. Every time we use the word, we are giving respect and praise to the white man who created the word. We are giving respect and praise to the millions of white men who raped our sisters and called them niggers while they violated them. We are giving respect and praise to the white man who forced the black man to whip his brother. He called both these men niggers as they destroyed each other.

I am told that we have reclaimed the word and spell it differently (nigga). Every dead slave owner buried in the ground is getting a big laugh out of us "reclaiming" a word they burned into our foreheads. We are a very creative people—let us make up a new word to replace nigger and stop giving respect and praise to our historic oppressor. We should make every effort to not drag this word into the 21st Century.

One of the best measures of cultural strength is the value particular groups place on the work of their artists. Are museums and companies created to preserve and protect the work? Who are the supporters and buyers of the art, the music, or the film? Are there efficient points of distribution for the artist to ensure fair compensation? Within the modern black diaspora, most artists of African ancestry would die without the support of non-Africans. It could be argued that one of the few groups

---

21   Cheikh Anta Diop, *The Cultural Unity of Black Africa* (Chicago: Third World Press), p. 225.

that do not celebrate contemporary African art (in its many forms) are contemporary Africans.

> It is the task of the poets, the artists, the writers, the men [and women] of culture, by blending into the daily round of suffering and denials of justice both memories and hopes, to create those great reserves of faith, those great storehouses of strength from which the people can draw courage in critical moments to assert themselves and to assault their future.[22]

Additional Resources

Books

Browder, Anthony T. (1992) *Nile Valley Contributions to Civilization.* Washington, D.C.: IKG.

Diop, Cheikh Anta (1974) *The African Origin of Civilization, Myth or Reality.* Westport, CT: Lawrence Hill Publishers.

Diop, Cheikh Anta (1990) *The Cultural Unity of Black Africa.* Chicago, IL: Third World Press.

Diop, Cheikh Anta (1987) *Precolonial Black Africa.* Westport, CT: Lawrence Hill Publishers.

Diop, Cheikh Anta (1991) *Civilization or Barbarism, An Authentic Anthropology.* Westport, CT: Lawrence Hill Publishers.

Garvey, Amy Jacques (1986) *The Philosophy & Opinions of Marcus Garvey.* Dover, MA: The Majority Press.

Karenga, Maulana (1989) *Selections from The Husia.* Los Angeles: The University of Sankore Press.

Van Sertima, Ivan (1993) *Golden Age of the Moors* (edited by). New Brunswick: Transaction Publishers.

Van Sertima, Ivan (1983) *Blacks in Science, Ancient and Modern* (edited by). New Brunswick: Transaction Publishers.

Van Sertima, Ivan (1992) *African Presence in Early America* (edited by). New Brunswick: Transaction Publishers.

Williams, Chancellor (1976) *The Destruction of Black Civilization.* Chicago: Third World Press.

Davidson, Basil (1992) *The Black Man's Burden.* New York: Times Books.

Diamond, Jared (1997) *Guns, Germs, and Steel: The Fates of Human Societies.* New York: W.W. Norton & Company.

---

22   Cheikh Anta Diop, *The Cultural Unity of Black Africa* (Chicago: Third World Press), p. 229.

CULTURAL & ECONOMIC REVITALIZATION

Aunk, Rudy (1998) *Doublespeak The Mini Book, America Needs A New Idea.* New York: NuuAunk, Inc.

World Wide Web
El-hajj Malik El-Shabazz (www.unix-ag.uni-lk.de/~moritz/malcolm)
Black Brazilians (www.igc.org/transafrica/DMoreira.html)
Ancient Greece (www.museum.upenn.edu./Greek_World/Intro.html)
Ancient Rome (www.exovedate.com/ancient_timeline_one.html)
Islam (www.muslimnet.net)
Christianity (www.azstarnet.com/~rgrogan/ce.htm)
Ancient Germanic Society (www.vinland.org/heathen/mt/wisdom.html)
Ethiopia (http://home.wxs.nl/~spaansen)
Nubia (www.umich.edu/~kelseydb/Exhibits/AncientNubia/AncientNubiaPressRelease.html)
Meroitic Queens (Www.msstate.edu/Archives/History/USA/Afro-Amer/women_in_nubia)
Ghana (http://asu.alasu.edu/academic/advstudies/1b.html)
Liberia (www.premier.net/~bethany/profiles/p_code4/1161.html)
Zimbabwe (www.zimweb.com/History.html)
Ebers and Edwin Smith Papyri (http://mason.gmu.edu/~mcrawfo1/health.html)
Ethiopia (www.ethiopians.com)
Jamaica (www.jamaica.com)
Senegal (www.earth2000.com/senegal)
The Honorable Marcus Mosiah Garvey (www.sscnet.ucla.edu/mgpp)
The Great Ida B. Wells (http://women.eb.com/women/articles/Wells-Barnett_Ida_Bell.html)
U.N.I.A. (www.unia-acl.org)
University of Paris (www.univ-paris5.fr)
University of Dakar (www.ucad.sn)
Booker T. Washington (www.otal.umd.edu/~mduvall/BTW.html)
Up From Slavery (www.msstate.edu/Archives/History/USA/Afro-Amer/bookertwash.txt)
The Maroons of Suriname (www.peabody.yale.edu/exhibits/maroons)
The Haitian Revolution (www.wsu.edu/~dee/DIASPORA/HAITI.HTM)
Pan African News Agency (www.africanews.org/PANA/news/)
Thabo Mbeki (www.mg.co.za/mg/news/97dec2/15dec-anc1.html)
Dr. Maulana Karenga (www.fsu.edu/~afroamhm/html/resident/karenga.html)
The Vatican (www.christusrex.org/www1/vaticano/0-Musei.html)

Mali (http://anthropologie.unige.ch/inagina/index.gb.html)
J. Edgar Hoover (www.crimelibrary.com/hoover/hoovermain.htm)
42 Declarations of Innocence (www.kemet.org)
African Languages (www.sil.org/ethnologue/countries/africa.html)
Languages for Foreign Travelers (http://travlang.com/languages/)
Language School (www.bostonlanguage.com)

Organizations
Afram Associates
> 271 West 125th Street, Suite 310
> Harlem, NY 10027
> 212.280.0996
> A public service communication agency founded in 1968. Its primary work is in the compilation, preservation, and authentication of the history of black people.

African American Museums Association
> 409 7th Street, N.W., Lower Level
> Washington, DC 20004
> 202.783.7744

African Heritage Studies Association
> P.O. Box 1633
> New York, NY 10037
> 212.795.2096

Association for the Study of Classical African Civilization (ASCAC)
> 3624 Country Club Drive
> Los Angeles, CA 90019
> 213.734.7551

DuSable Museum of African American History
> 740 East 56th Place
> Chicago, IL 60637
> 312.947.0600

Schomburg Center for Research in Black Culture
> 515 Malcolm X Boulevard
> New York, NY 10037
> 212.491.2200

STEP TWO
Environment of Love

I See Your Soul

I don't know where my dreams end and my life with you begins.
You are all that I ever dreamed for, prayed for, longed for.
I thought I was a whole person before I met you, but I was wrong
You have freed my soul from my cowardice and insecurity.
You're not with me tonight, but I see your soul.
My whole life has been a preparation to meet you.
What have I done to deserve you?
I see manhood on the horizon.
I know I was put on this earth to honor and love only you.
You're not with me tonight, but I see your soul in me.

Self Love

*I*n creating an environment of love, phase one begins with self. In nearly every instance, human beings who have unique facial or body characteristics are admired. They consider themselves better than the average person and they treasure their uniqueness. Examples include dimples, blue eyes, blond hair, and being taller than average. Unfortunately, this mentality has not been adopted by most black women and men. Our hair texture is a characteristic of people of African ancestry only. Our hair, like all the flowers of the earth, grows towards the Sun. A majority of black women take this blessing and destroy it nearly every month with chemicals and poisons. Many do so in hopes of attracting black men, who have stated a preference for straight hair.

Black women empower white women when they straighten their hair. Do we think that white people do not recognize our need to look more like them? Far too often the reason women straighten their hair is historic white supremacy. Black women will never out-white-woman the white woman. The more you try, the more the black man will treasure white women. If I ever have a family and I am blessed with a daughter, I would rather have my hands cut off than place poison on her beautiful hair.

The race concept in America grew out of 300 years of rape, exploitation, and mental torture that our people suffered. As African Americans, we carry much of that damage around in our hearts. As part of becoming the masters of our own destiny, each of us must forcefully remove the legacies of slavery from our minds. I continue to work to remove the intraracial baggage that was delivered to me throughout my life by family, friends, and society.

One of the most important ways to show love to yourself is by exercising and eating properly. The best exercise is that which provides you self-defense techniques, and improves, or at least maintains, your health. Just an hour of exercise a day cuts people's risk of stroke in half, doctors reported in a Harvard School of Public Health study. They reported in a 1997 study of 11,000 people, that those who did the equivalent of an hour's brisk walking five days a week, had a 46 percent lower risk of stroke than people who did not exercise. Even half that much exercise—the equivalent of a brisk half-hour walk most days—cuts the stroke risk by 24 percent.

"Not only did we find that physical activity is associated with reduced risk of stroke, but we also have some ideas as to how much and what type of activity might work best," Dr. I-Min Lee of the Harvard School of Public Health stated. "We found that doubling the effort showed an even greater reduction in stroke risk." Lee's team said they followed Harvard graduates who have been taking part in a study since 1962. The graduates were questioned in 1977 about how much exercise they got. Lee's team looked in 1990 to see how many had suffered strokes.

Those who exercised more were less likely to have strokes. When they took account of smoking, alcohol use, blood pressure, and diabetes—all known to affect stroke risk—Lee's team found exercise strongly protects people. "Walking, stair-climbing, and participating in moderately intense activities such as dancing, bicycling, and gardening were shown to reduce the risk of stroke," Lee said. "Light activity such as bowling and general housekeeping activity did not have the same effect."

Stroke is the third-biggest cause of death in the United States, after heart disease and cancer. Writing in the same journal, Pamela Duncan of the University of Kansas said she found exercise can help people recover from stroke. "For a long time, stroke has meant going to a nursing home to live out the rest of your life," Duncan stated. But her experiments on twenty stroke victims found intense exercise, three times a week, helped people recover lost motor skills like walking and coordination.[23]

Healthy eating is not difficult and can be managed in a cost effective manner. I have four principles that drive my eating habits.

- I avoid fast food in any form because it is slow poison for the body.
- I try to eat as much uncooked, unprocessed food as possible.
- I drink at least eight glasses of water per day.
- I try to incorporate as many of the vegetables and fruits that my ancestors ate in Western Africa into my diet.

Eating the right foods is a matter of life and death. For example, drinking milk from cows that have been treated with bovine growth hormone could cause cancer. A study of U.S. women published May 9, 1998, in the *Lancet* links insulin-like growth factor-1 (IGF-1) with breast cancer.[24] Earlier this year, a study linked IGF-1 to prostate cancer.[25] Prostate and breast cancers are major killers of men and women in the U.S. and in other industrialized countries. IGF-1 levels are now being artificially increased in much of the cows' milk being sold throughout the U.S. These new cancer studies raise serious questions about the wisdom of allowing IGF-1 levels to be raised in milk.

The May 1998 study found a seven-fold increased risk of breast cancer among pre-menopausal women younger than age fifty-one with the highest levels of IGF-1 in their blood. The prostate cancer study published in *Science* in January, 1998, found a four-fold increase in risk of prostate cancer among men with the highest levels of IGF-1 in their blood.[26] Thus, IGF-1 in blood is associated with larger relative risks for common cancers than any other factor yet discovered.

23 *American Heart Association, Stroke Journal*, Harvard School of Public Health study, October 1998.

24 Susan E. Hankinson and others, "Circulating concentrations of insulin-like growth factor I and risk of breast cancer," *Lancet* Vol. 351, No. 9113, 9 May 1998), pgs. 1393-1396.

25 June M. Chan and others, "Plasma Insulin-Like Growth Factor-I and Prostate Cancer Risk: A Prospective Study," *Science* Vol. 279, 23 January 1998, pgs. 563-566.

26 June M. Chan and others, "Plasma Insulin-Like Growth Factor-I and Prostate Cancer Risk: A Prospective Study," *Science* Vol. 279 (January 23, 1998), pgs. 563-566.

It is not clear from these studies whether IGF-1 causes these cancers, or whether elevated IGF-1 accompanies some other factor that causes these cancers. At the very least, researchers are hoping that measurements of IGF-1 will identify individuals at high risk of getting these cancers so that surveillance might be increased.[27]

IGF-1 is a powerful naturally-occurring growth hormone found in the blood of humans. Dairy cows injected with genetically-engineered bovine growth hormone (rBGH) give milk containing elevated levels of IGF-1, and the IGF-1 in milk can pass into the bloodstream of milk consumers. Cows' IGF-1 is chemically identical to that in humans. Ingested, IGF-1 would ordinarily be broken down in the stomach, but the presence of casein in milk prevents such breakdown.[28] Thus, these latest cancer findings raise important public health questions about the safety of milk from cows treated with bovine growth hormone.[29]

In efforts to generate higher profits, some food product companies have used chemicals to improve crop yields or extend the shelf life of many foods. These types of chemicals are to be avoided. The best way to avoid potentially harmful food chemicals is to eat certified organic foods. For infants and young children, organic foods are the best foods. Additionally, for infants, protein intake is critical for proper brain development.

The leading causes of death in the United States are heart disease and cancer. Vegetarians have much lower incidences of these diseases. According to the American Dietetic Association, scientific data suggest positive relationships between a vegetarian diet and reduced risk for several chronic degenerative diseases and conditions, including obesity, coronary artery disease, hypertension, diabetes mellitus, and some types of cancer. Vegetarian diets, like all diets, need to be planned appropriately to be nutritionally adequate.

According to the *Journal of the National Cancer Institute*, bowel cancer deaths and heart disease deaths in studied countries was directly proportional to those countries' per capita meat consumption. The

27 Environmental Research Foundation, *Rachel's Environment & Health Weekly* #598, 8 May 1998.
28 R.K. Rao and others, Luminal Stability of Insulin-Like Growth Factors I and II in Developing Rat Gastrointestinal Tract, *Journal of Pediatric Gastroenterology and Nutrition* Vol. 26, No. 2 (February 1998), pgs. 179-185.
29 Environmental Research Foundation, *Rachel's Environment & Health Weekly* #598, 8 May 1998.

number of deaths due to colon cancer, breast cancer, and prostate cancer was directly proportional to the average fat consumption. Vegetarians (especially vegans) have a much lower fat intake than non-vegetarians. Diabetes, another leading "disease of influence" in the U.S., is also found in the greatest degree among populations with high animal protein intake.

Unfortunately, black people are not only eating the wrong foods, but we are also participating in other acts of self-hatred. A 1998 study found that cigarette use among black high school students has jumped 80 percent since 1991.[30]

The nationwide survey found that, from 1991, when the Centers for Disease Control and Prevention (CDC) began the study, to 1997, smoking rates increased by one-third among all high school students. Forty-three percent used cigarettes, cigars, or smokeless tobacco in the month before the survey; a surprising 22 percent had smoked cigars during that time.[31]

But it was the sharp rise in black youths' smoking rates, which other studies showed to have dropped precipitously in the 1970s and 1980s, that health officials found most troubling. While white high school students still smoke at nearly twice the rate of Blacks, the gap has narrowed steadily in the 1990s, and some experts predict that it will close in the next decade.

The jump was particularly evident among young black males. In 1991, 14.1 percent of black male high school students smoked cigarettes; that figure climbed steadily throughout the six-year period, doubling to 28.2 percent by 1997. Among female black teenagers, smoking rates also rose, going from 11.3 percent in 1991 to 17.4 percent last year. Though their rate actually dropped from 1993 to 1995, it spiked most sharply in the most recent two years surveyed.[32]

In the search to explain the increase in smoking among black teenagers, a range of theories has evolved, from tobacco advertising in minority communities to the identification with entertainment idols who often appear smoking cigarettes, cigars, chewing tobacco, etc.

Teenagers themselves, and some experts who have studied adolescent smoking, add another: the decision to take up smoking because of a belief that cigarettes prolong the high of marijuana. Surveys show that

---

30 Sheryl Gay Stolberg, Smoking by Black Youths Is Up Sharply, Study Finds, *New York Times*, 3 April 1998.

31 Stolberg.

32 Stolberg.

Blacks begin smoking cigarettes later than white teenagers, but start using marijuana earlier.

In 1991, according to the CDC, 14.7 percent of students said they had used marijuana in the last thirty days; by 1995, the latest year for which data is available, that rate had jumped to 25.3 percent. Among white youth, the rate increased to 24.6 percent from 15.2. Among Hispanics, it shot up to 27.8 from 14.4, and among Blacks to 28.8 from 13.5, vaulting them from last place to first in marijuana usage by racial group.[33] As long as many of our youths' favorite music groups continue to celebrate the smoking of marijuana, I expect the numbers to continue to rise.

Black smokers have higher levels of nicotine in their blood- streams than white smokers, which may account for higher rates of tobacco-related diseases in Blacks. CDC research found that, although Blacks smoke on average fewer cigarettes than Whites, their blood levels of cotinine, a metabolized form of nicotine, were higher. CDC researchers said there is no clear reason for the difference. It could be related to smoking habits or biological differences in the way Blacks and Whites process nicotine in their bodies. Research showing higher retention of nicotine could help explain the lower rate of Blacks who quit smoking. The studies come at a time when the fastest growing population of new young smokers is young African Americans.[34]

To note, African American men represent 25 percent of all lung cancer victims. This number will clearly be rising in the future. We are literally eating and smoking ourselves to sickness and early death. Once we get sick, we do not stop eating and ingesting the various poisons; we take a pill to fix the problem.

A 1998 study argues that more than 100,000 Americans die in hospitals each year from adverse drug reactions. Millions more suffer serious injuries, such as heart irregularities and internal bleeding, as a result of allergic reactions or other complications from drugs that are often prescribed by doctors. The mortality and casualty statistics are even higher when researchers include cases in which patients got the wrong medication or improper doses. If the researchers are right, adverse reactions to drugs is the fourth leading cause of death in the U.S., after heart disease, cancer, and stroke.[35]

---

33   Jane Gross, "Youths Tie Tobacco Use to Marijuana," *New York Times*, 22 April 1998.

34   *Journal of The American Medical Association*, 7 July 1998.

35   "Controversial Study Finds Drug-Reaction Toll Is High," *Wall Street Journal*, April 1998.

If you want to make a change in the world, stay focused on yourself. You don't have to rebuild your community, just focus on self. When each one of us replaces our negativity and selfishness with love and respect, our families and communities will be transformed.

Family Love

Phase two of step two is focused on family. The ultimate success of any man or woman is the building of a loving family. We must begin to use the past as our guide. The quality of relationships between black women and men have reached an all-time low. At no time in our history has more bad will existed between us. Trust and respect are no longer taught and are often not practiced in the home. The standards of family excellence have dropped so low that a couple that creates a child and gets married is considered special. This issue has genocidal implications. If we continue on the present path, in less than one hundred years the majority of African American women, men, and children will be little more than nomadic parasites born into empty, love-starved and transient ghettos.

In 1910, 90 percent of African American children had their fathers at home; in 1960, the number was 80 percent; by 1990 the number had dropped to 38 percent.[36]

I am so saddened by the thought of millions of children being raised to adulthood without both of their parents. We can make excuses and develop illogical justifications for why children can grow up "just fine" in a single parent home. Talk show tirades about "I-don't-need-a-man-to-raise-my-child" are dysfunctional fairy tales. Judges who hear juvenile-delinquency cases state the single parent/family breakdown is the number one cause of violence by kids.[37]

There are millions of single parents working very hard to raise healthy families, but we must be honest. We will not survive as a race in America if we continue to ignore the principles of civilization, humanity, and family that our ancestors developed tens of thousands of years ago. Black boys are committing suicide in record numbers, increasingly pursuing various dysfunctional behaviors, and growing into adulthood with the value system of a ten year old. We must all become more active in helping young brothers and sisters end this painful game of

---

36 Jawanza Kunjufu, *Black Economics*, p. v.

37 *The National Law Journal* poll of 250 judges, conducted by Penn & Schoen Associates Inc., 1994.

monkey-see-monkey-do before the institution of marriage goes the way of no-sex-before-marriage in our communities.

Only a quarter of single parents receive the child support that is awarded them. More than half receive nothing at all. In all, $20 billion in child support goes unpaid every year, even though the Family Support Act contains new enforcement measures. Some of us complain about heartless politicians destroying the welfare system, but if black men would take responsibility for the children they help to create, we would not be as dependent on a system that is being dismantled.

In the past four decades, the traditions of marriage and family have been transformed among both Whites and Blacks. In 1950, 64 percent of black men age 14 or older were married, census data show. But by 1995, that proportion had fallen to 43 percent. The percentage of currently married white males in the same age category also dropped, but not nearly as much, from 68 percent in 1950 to 61 percent in 1995. Married black women are even rarer. Between 1950 and 1995, the percentage of black women 14 or older who were married fell from 62 percent to under 38 percent. Currently, 59 percent of all white women are married, down from 66 percent in 1950. Data collected by census researchers also suggest that fewer than 75 percent of black women can expect to marry sometime in their lives, compared with 90 percent of white women. Black divorce rates in the United States are among the highest in the world. Black marriages also may be more likely to end in divorce because married African American men and women are more likely to view life after a divorce more positively than do Whites.[38]

For women, an important alternative to welfare is marriage. Of the women who get off welfare, 35 percent got married.[39] Again, if the black man were to return to his historical role, we could increase the number of two-parent homes and, hopefully, reduce the number of our children in poverty. To note, if black women made better choices in men, this problem would also be reduced.

European Americans are the ethnic group with the most people in poverty, most illegitimate children, most unemployed men, and most arrests for serious crimes. And yet Whites have not had an "underclass" as such, because the Whites who might qualify have been scattered

---

38 Richard Morin, "A Crisis: Among Blacks, Major Changes in the Family Structure," *Washington Post*, 25 March 1998.

39 Department of Health and Human Services 1995.

among the working class.... But now the overall white illegitimacy rate is 22 percent. The figure in low-income, working class communities may be twice that. How much illegitimacy can a community tolerate? Nobody knows, but the historical fact is that the trendlines on black crime, dropout from the labor force, and illegitimacy all shifted sharply upward as the overall black illegitimacy rate passed 25 percent in the 1960s.[40]

What Makes a Great Woman?
- Respects mate in private and in public
- Invests constantly in personal intellect
- Shares sexuality as a gift, not a tool of manipulation
- Views femininity as a strength, not a weakness
- Supports her mate in all endeavors
- Measures love by actions and behavior, not material goods
- Understands life is not a television show
- Views motherhood as a blessing from God, not a burden
- Has financial security and flexibility
- Maximizes and maintains natural beauty

What Makes a Great Man?
- Takes personal responsibility for the success of his relationship
- Views women as a reflection of God
- Understands his mate is his best friend
- Has financial security and flexibility
- Sees commitment as a life goal
- Is a patient lover
- Wants one great woman, not five average women
- Places his relationship above himself
- Allows a woman to be herself
- Lives a life of honesty

Women and men could learn a few important lessons from certain chimpanzees in Africa. Pygmy chimpanzees or bonobo apes living in the Democratic Republic of the Congo create peaceful societies in which males and females share power. Similar chimpanzees throughout the world live in patriarchal groups in which males rape, beat, kill, and sometimes even drink the blood of their own kind. This research was published in 1997 by Houghton Mifflin in a book titled *Demonic Males*. The

---

40   Charles Murray, *Wall Street Journal*, "The Coming White Underclass," 29 October 1993.

book compares the violent patriarchal chimp societies to the matriarchal bonobo society and draws various conclusions for human society.

The authors', Richard Wrangham and Dale Peterson, theory is that human civilization would be more civilized if women seized more political power through elections and used it to counterbalance the male instinct to constantly define "enemies" and attack them. To make this advance, however, women must first abandon a tendency they share with female chimps to reward and select aggressive males as their mates.

The authors do not recognize the fact that many parts of ancient Africa were more civilized and developed because women were given/ took more power and authority in creating and recreating the civilization.

In the April 1994 issue of *Child Development Journal*, research was presented on children and poverty from several world-class American universities. The results of their studies provide important principles for parents raising children in poor environments. The news is not good for children born in poverty and raised in a single parent home. The most effective solution is to not start a family unit until you are mentally mature and financially secure.

The research highlighted that children's health and development had benefited significantly from the following protective caregiving factors:

- increased parental responsiveness;
- various toys and learning materials;
- variety of stimulation;
- greater parental acceptance of the child's behavior;
- a safe living area; and
- living in uncrowded conditions.

Children living in homes where three or more of these protective factors existed showed greater signs of resiliency by age three.[41]

Social support for parents living in poverty helps to alleviate problematic parental behavior, such as yelling and slapping children often and seldom praising or hugging. Perceiving a lack of social support may intensify feelings of hopelessness which in turn may influence the way poor parents interact with their children. Children in formal programs spent more time in academic and enrichment lessons and less time watching television and playing outside unsupervised than children in other types of daycare. They also spent more time in activities with peers and adults than children in the other care arrangements. Children who

41 *Child Development*, April 1994.

o participated in after-school academic activities had higher academic and conduct grades in school. The study also reported that participation in enrichment lessons was linked to better peer relations and emotional adjustment.[42]

The children from impoverished homes who started day-care before their first birthdays had higher reading scores than children from similar homes who did not attend day-care. For mathematics performance, children who went to a day-care center did better than children who didn't go to day-care at all, or children who went to other types of day-care, such as home-care. The benefit of center-based day-care for mathematics was only seen for children from impoverished homes.[43]

Poverty is a risk factor that can lead to delinquency, especially through its influence on parenting practices. As a response to stressful situations, parents in poverty often use erratic and harsh discipline which can cause children to model that behavior in the future and look to violence as a solution to their problems. However, they found families could overcome the effects of poverty and rear non-delinquent children through practice of healthy parenting techniques such as strong supervision and development of child/parent attachment.[44]

Differences in early language-learning experiences among children from poor, middle, and high socioeconomic backgrounds were found to predict language and academic performance up to ten years later in elementary school. Children whose early experiences led to smaller vocabularies by age three had lower language and reading-related performance through third grade.[45]

Recent research by three Texas-based academics is the first to examine linkages between the emotional climate of the family, social cognitive skills, and social competence for economically disadvantaged preschoolers. Among the researchers' specific findings are:

- Mothers who reported that they directed higher levels of anger toward the child and discouraged the child's expression of

42 Patricia Y. Hashima and Paul R. Amato, *Poverty, Social Support, and Parental Behavior.*

43 Margaret O'Brien Caughy, Janet A. Nipietro, and Donna N. Strobion, "Daycare Participation as a Protective Factor in the Cognitive Development of Low-Income Children."

44 Robert J. Sampson and John H. Laub , "Urban Poverty and the Family Context of Delinquency: A New Look at Structure and Process in a Classic Study."

45 Dale Walker, Charles Greenwood, Betty Hart, and Judith Carta, "Prediction of School Outcomes Based on Early Language Production and Socioeconomic Factors."

negative emotions had children who were less knowledgeable about anger.

- On the other hand, a positive emotional climate in the family was related to greater caregiving.
- Children with a greater understanding of emotions were also rated as more competent by their peers and they were more caring toward younger siblings.[46]

Children in lower socioeconomic classes are more likely than their peers to be the objects of harsh discipline, to observe violence in their neighborhoods and extended families, and to have more transient peer groups and, therefore, fewer opportunities for stable friendships. They receive less cognitive simulation in their home environment.[47]

Children have never been very good at listening to their elders, but they have never failed to imitate them.

—James Baldwin

We have to give our children, especially black boys, something to lose. Children make foolish choices when they have nothing to lose.

—Jawanza Kunjufu

Children who are truly loved...unconsciously know themselves to be valued. This knowledge is worth more than any gold... The feeling of being valuable—I am a valuable person—is essential to mental health and is a cornerstone of self-discipline. It is a direct product of parental love.

—M. Scott Peck

Community Love

As we look to rebuild our communities in phase three we need to recognize that, most often, we are our own worse enemy. A black slave told on Nat Turner, partially foiling his plans to destroy slavery in Virginia. A group of Blacks helped to destroy the Honorable Marcus Garvey. A handpicked black leader told the white world that slavery was a good thing because it gave us good work habits. Another group of Blacks

---

46 Pamela W. Garner, Diane Carison Jones, and Jennifer L. Miner, "Social Competence among Low-Income Preschoolers: Emotion Socialization Practices and Social Cognitive Correlates."

47 *Socioeconomic Status and Child Conduct Problems*, Kenneth A. Dodge, Gregory S. Pettit, and John E. Bates.

murdered Malcolm X. In 1996, a black business leader decided to begin selling hard liquor on his cable station. Another black businessman stated in a 1996 *New York Times Magazine* article that he prefers his dogs to black women. A number of Africans were involved in selling our sisters and brothers to Arabs and Europeans for pieces of fabric and non-working guns.

A challenge for most non-white communities in America is overcoming discrimination. Some obvious questions to ask are, What is discrimination? Are prejudice and racism the same thing? Is every member of the human race prejudiced? Is prejudice a bad thing? I am prejudiced. Every time I watch *Rocky,* I want Apollo Creed to knock out the white guy. I share more in common with Apollo than Rocky. He represents me, so I prefer him. I grew up in a white suburb of Boston. My neighbors were all crazy about Larry Bird. I thought he was a great player, but I was not a fan. I loved Julius Erving. I could see myself in Julius Erving–same skin color, same lips, same hair, etc.

Researchers at the University of Washington and Yale University have developed a new tool to measure people's "unconscious prejudice." They cautioned that results from the Implicit Association Test–that unconscious prejudice occurs in nine of ten people–could be disturbing, especially among those who consider themselves prejudice-free. The researchers, psychology professors Anthony Greenwald of the University of Washington and Mahzarin Banaji of Yale University, recently activated a World Wide Web site that allows people to test their own levels of inadvertent prejudice and stereotyping.[48]

Prejudice is preferring or disliking one person over another person based on a religious, gender, or racial commonality or difference. It is an individual choice. It happens all the time in the business world. Someone hires a person because they look like them or act like them. It can be wrong, but people mislabel it as racism. The damage that prejudice can cause is a function of power. If a prejudiced person has power and evil intentions, they can cause significant pain. Often, this person is more appropriately labeled a racist.

Am I racist because I want any children I might have to marry within my race? I do not think so. Many Europeans and Asians feel the same way. I do not view them as racists. It is a prejudicial view, but it is not a racist view. How could I not have this bias? When I see a black

---

48 The Associated Press, *Researchers Develop Prejudice Test,* October 11, 1998.

woman, I see my mother, my grandmother, and the Queens of ancient Africa.

Racism is prejudice with evil power. The African holocaust, the destruction of the Native American, the treatment of Japanese Americans during WWII, the destruction of European Jews, the starvation of the Irish, and the destruction of the Aborigines in Australia are examples of racism. I believe we are all prejudiced, but only a few of us ever become racists.

Are the prejudices that exist in the world due to class distinctions that are often defined by wealth and/or education or by race? I believe that race is a significant factor, but it has become apparent to me that class based on education is playing a larger and larger role in discrimination.

It was recently uncovered that the IRS targeted poor people for tax penalties because they believed they would not fight the penalties. I believe that there was a racial component to their discriminatory policy, but I also believe that they eagerly targeted the 60 percent of America's poor who are white.

In the summer of 1997, I experienced another example of class-over-race. I lived in Paris, France for the majority of 1997. When I first arrived in Paris, I did not know that I needed to carry my Metro (subway) ticket with me after I passed through the turnstile. During one trip, I was stopped by a group of subway police and forced to pay a 150FF fine for not carrying my ticket. These officers were quite rude to me. At the time, I had on shorts and a denim shirt. A week later, I ran into a similar police crew. This time they did not ask for my ticket. In fact, they moved out of my way as I walked through their checkpoint area. The only substantial difference was that I was in a business suit. Both groups of officers made assumptions about my social class based on my dress and adopted very different approaches in each situation.

Unfortunately, this increasing focus on class distinctions without an equally significant reduction in racial bias leaves the non-white poor in a very vulnerable position. Their best weapon is education. At present, the U.S. public school system is not equipped to provide the culturally-grounded, rigorous education that the poverty class desperately needs. It is no surprise that many of them choose to fight once they are backed into this difficult situation.

Additional Resources

Books

Three Initiates (1988) *The Kybalion.* Clayton, GA: Tri-State Press.

Afrika, Llaila O. (1994) *Nutricide–The Nutritional Destruction of the Black Race.*

Welsing, Frances Cress (1991) *The Isis Papers.* Chicago: Third World Press.

Vanzant, Iyanla (1996) *The Spirit Of A Man.* New York: Harper Collins.

Hesse, Hermann (1951) *Siddhartha.* New York: Bantam Books.

Peck, M. Scott (1978) *The Road Less Traveled.* New York: Simon & Schuster.

Moore, Thomas (1992) *Care Of The Soul.* New York: Harper Perennial.

Williamson, Marianne (1996) *A Return to Love–Reflections on the Principles of a Course in Miracles,* Reissue edition New York: Harper Collins.

Williamson, Marianne (1994) *A Woman's Worth* New York: Ballantine Books.

Ornish, Dean (1998) *Love & Survival–The Scientific Basis for the Healing Power of Intimacy* New York: HarperCollins.

World Wide Web

Better Eating (www.tiac.net/users/vrc/vrc.html)

American Dietetic Association (www.eatright.org)

Environmental Research Foundation (www.monitor.net/rachel/)

Centers for Disease Control and Prevention (www.cdc.gov)

James Baldwin (www.amassi.com/james.htm)

Jawanza Kunjufu (www.africanamericaimages.com)

M. Scott Peck (www.peoplesuccess.com/peck.htm)

Marianne Williamson (www.marianne.com)

Black Families (www.blackfamilies.com)

Child Development Journal (www.journals.uchicago.edu/CD)

Nat Turner (www.melanet.com/nat/)

Rocky, the Movie (www.toptown.com/hp/crs/rocky)

Boston, Mass. (www.boston.com)

Larry Bird (www.larrybird.com)

Julius Erving (www.nba.com/nbaat50/greats/erving.html)

Implicit Association Test (http://depts.washington.edu/iat/)

African Holocaust (www.tnp.com/holocaust)

Destruction of the Native American (www.word.com/gigo/whiteman)

Jewish Holocaust (www.fatherryan.org/holocaust)

Starvation of the Irish (www.ifgc.org)

Internal Revenue Service (www.irs.gov)

Paris, France (www.france.com)

STEP TWO

African Slavery (http://h-net2.msu.edu/~slavery/)

Organizations
Beyond Expectations
> Dept. of Psychology Northeastern Illinois University
> 5500 N. Street Louis Avenue
> Chicago, IL 60625
> 312.794.2568
> Designed to reduce violent behavior through community mentors who
> encourage the development of positive relationships and social
> principles that are thought to underlie altruistic behavior. The program's
> curriculum utilizes "The Rites of Passage"—a program designed to teach
> self-discovery using African history, culture, and customs.

Big Brothers/Big Sisters of America
> 230 North Thirteenth Street
> Philadelphia, PA 19107
> 215.567.7000
> National youth-service organization based on the concept of a
> One-to-One®relationship between an adult volunteer and an at-risk child.

Boys and Girls Clubs of America
> Gang Intervention Services
> 1230 W. Peachtree Street NW
> Atlanta, GA 30309
> 404.815.5764
> National movement providing youth development activities to more
> than 2,050,000 youth aged 6 to 18, with an emphasis on those from
> disadvantaged circumstances.

Children's Creative Response to Conflict (CCRC)
> Box 271, 523 N. Broadway
> New York, NY 10960
> 914.353.1796
> Dedicated to the training of teachers and students in the skills of
> conflict resolution, problem solving, peer mediation, bias awareness,
> cooperation, and affirmation.

Children's Defense Fund (CDF)
> 25 East Street, NW
> Washington, DC 20001
> 800.CDF.1200
> Committed to providing a strong and effective voice for all the children
> of America who cannot vote, lobby, or speak for themselves.

CULTURAL & ECONOMIC REVITALIZATION

Committee for Children
2203 Airport Way South, Suite 500
Seattle, WA 98134-2027
800.634.4449
Provides educational materials, original research, training, and community education for the prevention of child abuse and youth violence.

Girls Incorporated
30 E. 33rd Street
New York, NY 10016-5394
212.689.3700
Committed to helping girls become strong and bold. Girls ages 6 to 18, primarily from low income and minority backgrounds, participate in programs at almost 750 sites.

Healthy Family
1320 LaSalle Avenue, P.O. Box 9847
Hampton, VA 23670
604.727.1862
Provides parent education and child development services for families with children from the prenatal experience through age 12.

Head Start Association
1651 Prince Street
Alexandria, VA 22314
703.739.0875

The Kids Club, Dept. of Psychology
University of Michigan
580 Union Drive
Ann Arbor, MI 48109
313.763.3159
A ten-week preventive intervention group for 5- to 12-year-olds whose families have experienced domestic violence in the past year.

National Center for Injury Prevention and Centers for Disease Control and Prevention (CDC)
4770 Buford Highway, NE
Mail Stop F36
Atlanta, GA 30341
A national program to improve American health by preventing premature death and disability and reducing suffering and medical costs caused by non-occupational injury.

National Committee to Prevent Child Abuse
332 S. Michigan Avenue, Suite 1600
Chicago, IL 60604-4357
312.663.3520
Dedicated to preventing child abuse in all its forms.

New Mexico Center for Dispute Resolution
620 Roma NW, Suite B
Albuquerque, NM 87102
505.247.0571
Recognized as a national leader in developing and implementing
programs in mediation and conflict resolution for children, youth, and
families.

Oakland Men's Project
440 Grand Avenue, Suite 320
Oakland, CA 94610
510.835.2433
A nonprofit community education and organizing program dedicated to
teach about the causes of violence and the steps each of us can take to
stop abuses of power.

The Peace Education Foundation, Inc.
2627 Biscayne Boulevard
Miami, FL 33137
305.576.5075
Believes in teaching children the skill to find creative and nondestructive
ways to settle conflicts.

Self-Enhancement, Inc. (SEE)
2156 N.E. Broadway
Portland, OR 97232
503.249.1721
Provides in-school and after-school activities for 2nd to 12th grade at-risk
students. Also, SEE has a project designed to keep African-American
youth out of foster care.

Students Against Violence Everywhere (SAVE)
West Charlotte Senior High School
2219 Senior Drive
Charlotte, NC 28216
704.343.6060
Student-initiated program that teaches elementary and secondary school
students how to resolve conflict among themselves, and gun safety
awareness

Study Circles Resource Center (SCRC)
P.O. Box 203
Pomfret, CT 06258
203.928.2616
Fosters grassroots participation in the democratic process by promoting
small group, democratic, highly participatory discussions known as
study circles. SCRC has published Confronting Violence in Our
Communities.

CULTURAL & ECONOMIC REVITALIZATION

Supporting Adolescents with Guidance and Employment (SAGE)
Center for Social Research and Policy Analysis
Research Triangle Institute, P.O. Box 12194
Research Triangle Park, NC 27709
919.541.6252
A program that targets black male adolescents in Durham, NC. Overall goal is to prevent or reduce the incidence of violence and other high-risk behavior among participants.

Teens on Target (TNT)
3012 Summit Avenue, Suite 3670
Oakland, CA 94609
510.444.6191
Goal is to train urban youth to become health advocates for violence prevention. Mission is to reduce violent deaths and injuries, especially from firearms.

Victim Service School Mediation & Violence Prevention
2 Lafayette Street
New York, NY 10007
212.577.1370
Founded in 1978, it is the largest victim assistance organization in the country.

YouthBuild Boston
173A Norfolk Avenue
Roxbury, MA 02119
617.445.8887
Nationally recognized youth development agency that involves unemployed, disenfranchised young people in renovating abandoned buildings as affordable housing while offering them a second chance to gain education, skills, and personal support.

STEP THREE
Educational Excellence

Some Days

Some days I hope to never see you again
Other days only the thought of you allows me to survive another
Some days I walk on air like a billowing cloud traveling
around a mountain peak
Other days I crawl like a snail without a shell in the desert heat
Some days I stagger around town with my fist balled up looking to strike
Other days I drift from place to place hoping to be liked
Some days I know that I have taken the wrong path
Other days I wonder if my success will last
One day I will find the person I must become,
to be the person that I know I once was

Vision

*P*hase one of educational excellence is centered around vision. One of
the greatest destroyers of vision is excuses. I have little respect for
people who use excuses as a way of life. Unfortunately, I find people of
African ancestry making far too many excuses about far too many things.
When we are presented with factual information that Africans sold other
Africans to the Europeans as slaves, we make excuses for those cowards.
When we are presented with the gross shortcomings of too many African
American men, we make excuses for their behavior. When other disen-
franchised groups work together in trust and respect and build vibrant
cultural and economic systems in the U.S., we make excuses why we have
not done the same. The easiest thing in the world to do is make an excuse.
Anyone can do it, a three-year-old child or a forty-year-old man. It takes

no discipline, no practice, and you can use them over and over again. An excuse is like a fart: anyone can do it and they all stink.

Once the black man would risk death to defend the honor of the black woman. Now, too many of us spend our days destroying our sisters' honor. What happened? Community desertion and television were major contributors to creating a new, more ignorant, more selfish black man over the last thirty years. Mass television presented images that guaranteed you could find dysfunctional examples and images of black people. This was juxtaposed against images of loving, thoughtful, heroic white people. This, by itself, was not the killer. Most non-white people are presented as ugly stereotypes on television and film. At the same time that television was educating us to be dysfunctional, many of the role models of our historic communities were leaving to go live in white communities. One-way integration had arrived. In a very short period of time, this left our communities without the healthy black men and women and families that once lived next door to the single mother or the unemployed man. With the departure of the positive and healthy, ignorant people began to educate ignorant people how to be more ignorant. Television provided a reinforcement for the ignorance and presented the supposed rewards you would receive for being ignorant. Standards of acceptable behavior are falling every day. Our vision of ourselves is being destroyed. Although African Americans represent 12 percent of the U.S. population, we are junkies for simple-minded entertainment:

- represent more than 25 percent of movie theater revenues;
- are four times as likely to subscribe to a premium pay television service versus Whites;
- spent $2.25 billion on cable television subscriptions with 61 percent spending $36.00+ per month versus 24 percent for Whites; and
- watch nearly 50 percent more television (73 hours per week) than Whites.

A 1998 study looked at television through the eyes of children. Blacks and Hispanics are not always encouraged by what they see on television. Children more often associate positive qualities—financial and academic success, leadership, intelligence—with white characters, and associate negative qualities—lawbreaking, financial hardship, laziness, goofy behavior—with minority characters. Seventy-one percent of all children said the role of boss is usually played by someone who is white, while 59 percent said the role of criminal is typically played by Blacks.[49] Many of us feel powerless to affect change in our world. Each of us can stop supporting and viewing images of ourselves that perpetuate helplessness, sexism, and dysfunction.

Parents of girls must be doubly careful of sexism in the classroom. It can also destroy vision. In an article from the *Wall Street Journal* on December 4, 1994, a "progressive" kindergarten in New Jersey was exposed for its sexist student awards. The boys in the school received the following awards:

- very best thinker;
- most eager learner;
- most imaginative;
- most enthusiastic;
- most scientific;
- best friend;
- Mr. Personality;
- hardest worker; and
- best sense of humor.

The girls received awards that were superficial and almost irrelevant:

- all-around sweetheart;
- sweetest personality;
- cutest personality;
- best sharer;
- best artist;
- biggest heart;
- best manners;
- best helper; and
- most creative.

In June 1997, Dr. Asa G. Hilliard III delivered the keynote address at the sixth annual NAEYC National Institute for Early Childhood Professional Development. Dr. Hilliard looked beyond traditional educational concepts and challenged "bell-shaped curve" thinking in his address. He urges educators and caregivers to adopt proven, if unorthodox, methods to facilitate learning for all children by encouraging natural development within a supportive and caring environment. His address provided five methods of how to release the genius shared by virtually all humans.

---

49   Children Now Survey March 1998, A Different World.

The first model is based on the work of Shinichi Suzuki, a self-taught teacher best known for an approach to music teaching in which all children succeed. Suzuki's philosophy of learning is a combination of perseverance, energy, patience, and repetition coupled with a superior environment that provides continual exposure to masterful examples, noting that "humans instinctively adapt to any environment...inspiration and interest are acquired involuntarily from exposure. A superior environment has the greatest effect in creating superior human beings."

The second model is drawn from *Kandeze–the Congo Art of Baby Sitting* by K. Kia Bunseki Fu-Kiau of the former Zaire. Kandeze is a Zairian term meaning to nurture the child and the environment. Like Suzuki, Fu-Kiau believes the character issue of the individual is the key. Kandeze involves the elders in the community in an active program of storytelling and singing which transfers into the child's own language the songs, stories, legends, and games. These contain the lessons in character, the meaning of life, the role of the community. Everyone, men and women, must participate in the process and much of the program's success is attributed to the quality of relationships, which develop, and to the extensive repetition that occurs as a natural part of the process.

Hilliard's third model was the work of Erik Erikson, founder of the Erikson Institute in Chicago. He described Erikson's work as providing a map of Human Development to nurture a sense of "I can do it myself," through stages of: I can begin this; Who am I; I see you; Generalization; and Integrity.

The fourth model presented came from Marion Lundy-Dobbert, et al., at the University of Minnesota and their observations on the learning behavior of primates. Like humans, primates learn by observation and modeling, through social experience, through social conflict, and through play; particularly play in which there exists a slight arousal but open emotional state, much repetition, and a free combination of physical, cognitive, and behavioral opportunity.

The fifth model draws on the work of Augusta Mann with Wade Nobles at the San Francisco State University, who conduct highly regarded "Power Learning Conferences" showing techniques to help the brain make connections coupled with exercises to give the connections meaning. "Deep meanings are what human beings live for...and development requires nurture, not nature."

Summarizing the common elements of these five models with the assertion that character is determined by the environment that we create for children, Hilliard exhorted leaders to:

- destroy doubt;
- touch the spirit;
- focus on child's character (*who, not what*);
- build bonds with the child and with each other, and;
- adopt the expectation that every child in their care will succeed and become a noble human being.

Home Education

Phase two takes place in the most important place of learning, the home. Parents must incorporate the local library into a child's regular activities. If you take your child to the video store more often than the bookstore/library, you are likely cheating your child.

An important activity for parents is to take their children on field trips to the best Universities in their city. Place a vision of positivity and excellence in front of your child. If you are not what you want your child to be, then find someone who is. If you want your child to be a doctor, then she must see doctors. If you let the streets be the role model for your child, you will likely get a street hustler.

As a parent, you should supplement a reading list at school with books that properly reinforce historical identity and self-worth. It is equally important that you review all your child's reading material to ensure that self-hatred is not being taught in the school. School is a horrible substitute parent.

School

The final phase is focused on school. The answer to improving the public school system is not simply more money. Many states with consistently high test scores spend well below average per pupil on education. In contrast, the states that spend the most have among the lowest test scores. Parental involvement is what improves schools most.

Calls for more computers in the classroom should be guided by a recent nationwide study in the U.S. The study examined the use of computers in schools and concluded that the $5 billion being spent each year on educational technology is actually hurting children in many cases because the computers aren't being put to good use.

The study of nearly 14,000 fourth and eighth graders showed that students who spent more time on computers in school actually scored worse on math tests than students who spent less time with computers. The students' lower scores appeared to be caused by the ineffective but widespread use of computers for repetitive math drills, instead of simulations and real-life applications of math concepts which are computer uses that seem to improve math scores.

The research by New Jersey-based Educational Testing Service offers the first solid evidence of what works and what doesn't when computers are used in the nation's classrooms. While educators have known for some time that having PCs in the classroom was useful in teaching computer use itself, several earlier studies have provided no conclusive evidence that the new technology was any better as a tool than pencils and paper in teaching children to read, write, and do mathematics.

Overall, the new study found computers can be an important learning tool, but only in certain circumstances and when teachers are well-skilled in their use. The study's author, Harold Wenglinsky, also identified a troubling racial element in the varying use of computers. His work indicated that black children use computers to learn mathematics somewhat more often than white children, but that Blacks are far more likely than Whites to engage in the less useful drill and practice exercises. Students whose teachers had been trained in teaching with computers did better than students whose teachers lacked such training. Low-income and black students were the least likely to have teachers who exploited all of the computers' possible uses.[50]

The value of learning in environments where you are a majority of the student body is clear. Historically, black colleges only have 17 percent of black college students, yet they produce nearly 40 percent of the graduates. Jawanza Kunjufu points out that 75 percent of African Americans who go on to receive their MA or Ph.D. at majority white school received their undergraduate education at majority black schools.

Recent revelations by the national press that nearly all the founding fathers of America owned enslaved human beings highlights the fundamental dilemma of Africans in modern America and directly effect our

---

50 Jay Mathews, "Study Faults Computers' Use in Math Education Repetitive Drills, Lower Scores Linked," *Washington Post*, 30 September 1998; Page A03.

childrens' interest in education.[51] Quaker William Penn, the founder of Pennsylvania, owned enslaved people. He once remarked slaves were the best servants because they were permanent. Andrew Johnson had enslaved people in his home in Washington D.C., while he was Abraham Lincoln's vice president. Andrew Jackson placed an ad seeking the recapture of an enslaved person who had escaped his evil grip and offered an extra $10 for every 100 lashes the captor gave the enslaved person, up to $300. Half the signers of the Declaration of Independence were slave owners.

How credible are the signers of the Declaration of Independence as founding fathers or even human beings? How should I judge their role as the tormentors of my people? Some black leaders suggest that you must accept the norms of society at that time and measure the people based on their overall contributions to society. Benjamin Franklin owned enslaved people for thirty years and sold them at his general store, but he was the first American multi-genius. I consider these people to be criminals who should have spent most of their lives in prison for their crimes against humanity. As long as America ignores these deep contradictions in its history, we will not be a whole nation.

Many scholars have worked to create a teaching platform that offers students an opportunity to see themselves. One of the leaders is Dr. Molefi Kete Asante. Dr. Asante's definition of multiculturalism provides a wonderful foundation for understanding the importance of multiculturalism, not just in education, but for all of society.

The idea of multiculturalism in the academia signals evolution in thought about education and is an indication of a social consciousness that leaps toward national unity. This is so, despite the fact that many people have disparaged the idea for a variety of reasons.

Multiculturalism in education is the quality of creating and sustaining curricula, academic activities, programs, and projects that actively enhance respect for all human cultures. Seeking a multicultural academy does not portend the disuniting of America; instead, it suggests the possibility that a multiplicity of self-respecting and other-respecting cultures could co-exist in a more perfect union. In fact, the only way that diverse cultures can co-exist for long is on the basis of such mutual appreciation and respect. Thus, multiculturalism in academia is one way to support the objective of an effective education for the 21st Century,

---

51 *USA Today*, 9 March 1998.

when colleges and universities will be far more diverse than they are today. However, it is not diversity itself that should encourage multiculturalism, but our commitment as human beings to the fullest possible appreciation of other cultures. It does not matter whether the college is located in an all-white town in Iowa, the imperatives for multiculturalism are based on the concrete values of human cultural experiences.[52]

It has been said since the beginning of time, "education pays." As we enter the 21st Century, the new slogan should be "ignorance kills." Real wages for the least skilled workers have declined 23.3 percent since 1979, making it harder than ever to work one's way out of poverty. Wages for those with more education and skills, in contrast, have risen.[53] The earnings gap between black male college and high school graduates has quadrupled since 1990.[54]

Additional Resources

Books
Asante, Molefi (1988) *Afrocentricity.* Trenton, NJ: Africa World Press.
West, Cornel (1993) *Race Matter.* Boston: Beacon Press.
Steele, Shelby (1990) *The Content of Our Character.* New York: HarperPerennial.
Murray, Albert (1996) *The Blue Devils of Nada.* New York: Vintage Books.

World Web Wide
Historically Black Colleges (www.uncf.org)
USA Today (www.usatoday.com)
Declaration of Independence (www.law.indiana.edu/uslawdocs/declaration.html)
Dr. Molefi Kete Asante (www.asante.com)
Wall Street Journal (www.wsj.com)
Shinichi Suzuki (http://suzukimethod.org)

---

52 *Academe,* Bulletin of the American Association of University Professsors, May/June 1996.
53 Bureau of Labor Statistics, 1996.
54 Bureau of Labor Statistics, 1996.

STEP THREE

Organizations
Beacons
New York City Dept. of Youth Services
44 Court Street
Brooklyn, NY 11201
718.403.5359
School-based community centers, managed by nonprofit
community-based organizations, that work collaboratively with school
boards, principals, teachers, and community advisory boards of parents.
Center for Media Literacy (CML)
19625 Shenandoah Street
Los Angeles, CA 90034
310.559.2944
The CML mission is to help children and adults prepare for living and
learning in a global media culture by translating media literacy research
and theory into practical information, training, and educational tools
for teachers, youth leaders, parents, and childcare givers.
The Community Board Program
1540 Market Street, Suite 490
San Francisco, CA 94102
415.552.1250
A nationally recognized conflict resolution organization, established in
San Francisco in 1976. Work involves the combination of classroom
conflict resolution curricula (K-12) and student-to-student peer
mediation programs.
Education Development Center, Inc. (EDC)
55 Chapel Street
Newton, MA 02160
617.969.7100
Dedicated to promoting human development through education and
through a wide range of projects, EDC works to address educational,
health, and social problems.
Educators for Social Responsibility (ESR)
23 Garden Street
Cambridge, MA 02138
617.492.1764
Its primary mission is to help young people develop a commitment to
the well-being of others and to making a positive difference in the world.
National Association for Mediation in Education (NAME)
205 Hampshire House, Box 33635, UMASS
Amherst, MA 01003
413.545.2462
Promotes the development, implementation, and institutionalization of
school and university-based conflict resolution programs and curricula.

CULTURAL & ECONOMIC REVITALIZATION

National School Safety Center (NSSC)
4165 Thousand Oaks Boulevard, Suite 290
Westlake Village, CA 91362
805.373.9977
NSSC is mandated to focus national attention on solutions to problems that disrupt the educational process.

The National Society of Black Engineers
Membership Services Department
1454 Duke Street
Alexandria, VA 22314-3429
703.549.2207 ext. 210
NSBE's mission is to increase the number of culturally responsible black engineers who excel academically, succeed professionally, and positively impact the community.

Youth Education and Support Services (YESS)
Battered Women's Alternatives
P.O. Box 6406
Concord, CA 94524
510.229.0885
Provides dating, family, and community violence prevention and intervention services for youth throughout Contra Costa County and national training for professionals.

STEP FOUR
Community Empowerment

Box

It is bad enough that you live in a box.
A box that says violence is the best way to get respect.
A box that says educational excellence is something for other people.
A box that says it is cool to disrespect women.
The worst truth is that you do not own the box,
nor did you build the box.

Community Service

*P*hase one in community empowerment is community service. The theme is: you are the customer of your government; demand the best. Police protection is one area in which urban America has received poor service. From police supporting and selling drugs in our community, to false arrests and brutality, many police departments of the United States of America receive low marks. One solution to this problem is for more people of African ancestry to become police officers and effect change from within.

Garbage collection and clean streets require the same diligence that many communities are taking towards police brutality. Call your elected officials every time your garbage is not properly collected. Graffiti is also garbage, not art, when it is illegally painted on someone else's property. A polluted, dirty community is the worst environment for children.

Crime Prevention

Phase two is focused on crime prevention. Most of the crimes in urban America are perpetrated by self-hating individuals. If we are able to implement steps one and two of the CER model, crime will be reduced. What is the best way to reduce crime? A key question is who is in prison?

- 46 percent did not complete high school[55]
- 49 percent were under the influence of alcohol, other drugs, or both during crime[56]
- 43 percent of the women were sexually or otherwise physically abused in their past[57]
- More than 70 percent of the juveniles in state reformatories come from homes without fathers[58]
- Sixty percent of rapists and 72 percent of adolescent murderers grew up without fathers[59]
- Children from single-parent homes are 40 percent more likely to repeat a grade in school and 70 percent more likely to be expelled[60]
- The daughters of single parents are more than twice as likely to have a child out-of-wedlock.[61]

We can reduce crime by ending the cycle of fatherless homes that began in the 1960s. We can also reduce crime by reducing our use and the availability of drugs and alcohol. Alcohol abuse is a factor in nearly 40 percent of violent crime in the United States, despite declines in alcohol consumption and other offenses usually tied to drinking. Virtually all of the offenders were men, and most of them were drunk when they committed the crime. Some were almost three times over legal intoxication blood-alcohol limits and were described as heavy drinkers.[62]

In a January 1994 published report titled, "Evaluation of the Five Oaks Neighborhood Stabilization Plan," the winning concept of neighborhood stabilization (or crime reduction) is detailed. Neighborhood Stabilization is the intended result of the "Defensible Space" theory, which is based mainly on the concept of neighborhood ownership. Using physical barriers, such as street and alley closure, cul-de-sacs are created within typical grid patterned neighborhoods. These mini-neighborhoods

55 Bureau of Justice Statistics, 1993.

56 Bureau of Justice Statistics, 1993.

57 Bureau of Justice Statistics, 1993.

58 Bob Dole and J.C. Watts, Jr., *The Wall Street Journal*, A New Civil Rights Agenda, 27 July 1995.

59 Dole and Watts, Jr.

60 Dole and Watts, Jr.

61 Dole and Watts, Jr.

62 U.S. Department of Justice, April 1998 Survey.

are designed to create a space in which neighbors can "defend" themselves against overwhelming through-traffic and the problems associated with it. Modern subdivisions have pro-actively used cul-de-sacs and limited access for these very same reasons. According to Mr. Newman (the creator of the Defensible Space Theory), a constant and increasing flow of unwanted traffic has the following effects on a neighborhood:

- it reduces contact between neighbors;
- it increases crime (especially crimes of opportunity such as burglary);
- it decreases the amount of investment people will make in their homes and, therefore, the neighborhood; and
- it decreases housing values.

Defensible space is a model for residential environments which inhibits crime by creating the physical expression of a social fabric that defends itself. All the different elements which combine to make a defensible space have a common goal—an environment in which latent territoriality and sense of community in the inhabitants can be translated into responsibility for ensuring a safe, productive, and well-maintained living space. The potential criminal perceives such a space as controlled by its residents, leaving the intruder easily recognized and dealt with. On the one hand, this is target hardening—the traditional aim of security design as provided by locksmiths. But it should also be seen in another light. In middle-class neighborhoods, the responsibility for maintaining security has largely been relegated to the police. Upper-income neighborhoods, particularly those including high-rise apartment buildings, have supplemented police with doormen, a luxury not possible in other neighborhoods.[63]

Ninety billion dollars are spent each year on police, courts, and prisons. Sixty-five billion is spent on alarms, private guards, and security systems. Urban decay, which is the cost of lost jobs and fleeing residents, costs $50 billion per year. Property loss, defined as the value of stolen goods, is $45 billion. Annual medical care for crime victims is $5 billion. The economic value of lost and broken lives is estimated at $170 billion. Total crime costs in the United States of America are $425 billion per year.[64]

---

63 Oscar Newman, *Crime Prevention Through Urban Design*, 1973, pg. 3.
64 "The Economics of Crime," *Business Week*, 13 December 1993.

Several gun buy-back programs have been successful in taking deadly firearms off the street. Contact your local politicians and demand a buy-back program. In March 1998, the Newark Police Department concluded a month-long program to buy back weapons from local gun owners It collected a total of 653 firearms at a cost of $47,725. The program retrieved 358 pistols and revolvers, 107 automatic handguns, 104 rifles, 70 shotguns, and 14 assault rifles, including one AK-47.

Ballistics tests determined that at least thirty-six of the weapons were fired during the commission of a crime. Though the program promises anonymity making it impossible for the police to prosecute people who return guns, it at least succeeded in taking the weapons off the street.

Political Power and Influence

The final phase in step four is political power. Voting is critical. If 90 percent of people of African ancestry voted in America, we would wield substantially more influence and power. To further increase that power we must not allow any one political party to take our votes for granted. Additionally, we must understand that political power and influence is not a cure-all. If the United States America had a President, Vice President, and Speaker of the House of African ancestry, we would still have decaying values and a crumbling family structure.

Black people have become far too kind and forgiving of our politicians. We hire/elect them based on specific promises and platforms and then we allow them to forget about delivering results. Many are excellent at protesting, but poor on implementing solutions. Most of our public schools are horrible. Many of our communities are less safe every year. Are your politicians improving your quality of life or just their own?

Push your politicians to relax occupational licensing requirements and decrease taxes on low-wage workers. Over 400 occupational licensing laws limit who can apply for nearly ten percent of all U.S. jobs. Push your politicians to secure funding for community day care centers that train and hire staff from the community. If your community has been in a continual decline, vote those inactive and inept individuals out of office.

Additional Resources

Books

Drake, St. Clair (1993) *Black Metropolis: A Study of Negro Life in a Northern City*, Chicago: University of Chicago Press

Fanon, Frantz (1963) *The Wretched Of The Earth.* New York: Grove Press.

Freedman, Samuel (1993) *Upon This Rock.* New York: Harper Collins.

El-Shabazz, El-hajj Malik (1964) *The Autobiography of Malcolm X.* New York: Ballantine Books.

World Wide Web

Police Brutality (www.bwbadge.com)

Organizations

Ashoka Innovators for the Public
   1700 North Moore Street, Suite 1920
   Arlington, VA 22209-1903
   703.527.8300
   Empowering social entrepreneurs

Boston Violence Prevention Program
   Health Promotion Program for Urban Youth Dept. of Health and Hospitals
   Massachusetts Avenue, 2nd Floor
   Boston, MA 02118
   617.534.5196
   Provides programs on reducing violence among adolescents using a multifaceted, multidisciplinary approach grounded in public health practice that focus on primary and secondary prevention program strategies.

The Center to Prevent Handgun Violence
   1225 Eye Street, NW, Suite 1100
   Washington, DC 20005
   202.289.7319
   National education, legal action, and research organization founded in 1983 to educate Americans about the scope of gun violence and to prevent further bloodshed.

Center for the Studies and Prevention of Violence (CSPV)
   University of Colorado at Boulder
   IBS #9, Campus Box 442
   Boulder, CO 80309-0442
   303.492.1032
   Committed to building bridges between researchers, practitioners, and policy-makers working to understand and prevent violence, particularly adolescent violence.

The Child Witness to Violence Project
Boston City Hospital
818 Harrison Avenue
Boston, MA 02118
617.534.4244
Addresses the needs of children who are exposed to violence. Offers counseling and advocacy services to children eight years old and under who have witnessed violence.

Coalition to Stop Gun Violence (CSGV)
100 Maryland Avenue, NE
Washington, DC 20002-5625
202.544.7190
Its goal is the orderly elimination of most handguns and assault weapons from the U.S.

The 1999 Congressional Handbook
Pub. Fulfillment, U.S. Chamber
1615 H. Street, NW
Washington, D.C. 20062-2000
The 1999 Congressional Handbook containing addresses, phone numbers, and photos of each member, plus staff listings, committee assignments, and other information. To order a copy, send $7.50.

The HELP (Handgun Epidemic Lowering Plan) **Network**
Children's Memorial Medical Center
2300 Children's Plaza, Box #88
Chicago, IL 60614
312.880.3826
A resource center for organizations and individuals concerned with the growing epidemic of death, disability, and suffering caused by handguns.

The Houston Violence Prevention Project
Houston Dept. of Health and Human Services
Chronic Disease and Injury Prevention Program
8000 N. Stadium Drive
Houston, TX 77054
713.794.9911
Five-year community demonstration project that combines school-based peer leader education with parenting and community involvement activities for neighborhood adults.

Last Chance Ranch
Florida Environmental Institute
P.O. Box 406
Venus, FL 33960
813.465.6508
Nonprofit juvenile rehabilitation program designed to work with the most serious juvenile offenders in the state of Florida.

Mothers Against Violence
154 Christopher St., Second Floor
New York, NY 10014
212.255.5484
A coalition of New York City women who are working to mobilize
residents, public officials, professionals, and youth to address the
epidemic of youth violence.

Movement for Chhange
National Black Theatre
Harlem, NY 10027
914.969.8541
A youth movement created by Minister Conrad Muhammad to mold
youth leaders and register young people to vote.

National Crime Prevention Council (NCPC)
1700 K Street NW, 2nd Floor
Washington, DC 20006-3817
202.466.6272
The principal mission of NCPC is to enable people to prevent crime
and build safer, more caring communities.

The Pacific Center for Violence Prevention
San Francisco General Hospital
Building One, Room 300
San Francisco, CA 94110
415.285.1793
Its goals include shifting society's definition of youth violence from a
law enforcement model to include a public health model that addresses
societal influences contributing to youth violence.

PACT (Policy, Action, Collaboration, Training) **Violence Prevention Project**
75 Santa Barbara Road
Pleasant Hill, CA 94523
510.646.6511/510.374.3797
A collaboration of the Contra Costa County Health Services
Department Prevention Program and ten West County
community-based agencies.

Parents of Murdered Children (POMC)
lODE. 8th Street, B-41
Cincinnati, OH 45202
513.721.5683
Dedicated to providing support to those who have lost a loved one to
violence.

The Rape, Abuse & Incest National Network (RAINN)
A 24 hour national hot line for instant referrals to local organizations
1.800.656.HOPE

Save Our Sons and Daughters (SOSAD)
2441 West Grand Boulevard
Detroit, MI 48208
313.361.5200
A nonprofit, grassroots organization in Detroit that was founded in
January 1987 by Clementine Barfield when her two sons were shot, one
of them fatally.

The Task Force on Violent Crime
614 Superior Avenue W, Suite 300
Cleveland, OH 44113-1306
216.523.1128
Serves as a catalyst in utilizing the full resources of the greater Cleveland
community to develop and provide comprehensive programs to reduce
violent crimes.

Violence Policy Center (VPC)
1300 N Street, NW
Washington, DC 20005
202.783.4071
National educational foundation that conducts research on firearms
violence in the U.S. and works to develop violence reduction policies
and proposals.

Voter's Research Hotline
800.622.SMART

STEP FIVE
Economic Development

There's Something Wrong in Harlem

There's Something Wrong in Harlem
That Mother called her five-year-old son an asshole
There is no such thing
Goodbye innocence
Where are the black businesses?
Who's the white guy I see on every other corner?
Oh that's Jesus
How did you find Jesus? Which plantation?
There's Something Wrong in Harlem

It's 10:00 pm and I see two-year-old children playing in the gutters
Gutters are for washing things away
Potential, dreams, a future, a community
If your skirt was any higher it would be a scarf
You have to be a good woman before you can attract a good man
Is there a law against black couples up here?
McDonald's in the lobby of a Hospital
White Castle, KFC—all negroes welcomed
There's Something Wrong in Harlem

Girl I want to get with you
Well not really, you know
Booty call, I'm a player
You be Foxy Brown and I'll be the Stone Faced Killa
Tonight you be having my baby
Tomorrow my Daddy gets out of prison
Mr. Garvey we need your help
There's Something Wrong in Harlem

Government Free Income

*P*hase one of economic development is government-free income. We must begin the process of economic development by reducing our need for government aid. Executing the Cultural and Economic Revitalization model will bring more jobs into our community. About 1.7 million jobs are lost to the inner city because its residents don't buy from each other. These purchasing patterns prevent the formation of black capital. The result is starkly presented in 1990 census figures from California: 1 of every 10 Koreans is a business owner, 1 of every 15 Whites, 1 of every 22 Hispanics, and 1 of every 67 Blacks.[65]

Jim Brown, arguably the greatest athlete of the 20th Century, has articulated on many occasions what we need for lasting economic development. In a February 7, 1995, interview on The Charlie Rose Show he stated, "We are used to being civil rights workers. Dr. King was a wonderful man, but his concepts were totally inadequate for this country. We must use the rules of the Jewish community; we must use the rules of the Korean community. *Every community that has advanced has done so by coming together itself first, defining its own economics, defining its own community, and then dealing on an equal level with the community at large.*"

There is no excuse for check cashing operations to exist in the black community. Since most banks with "urban" branches offer free checking accounts. Understand that every time we process a check and the owners of these operations take a portion of your money just to cash the check, that non-black-owned operation is laughing at us.

Examination of wealth data highlights the capital weaknesses of the black community. Whites possess over eleven times as much median net worth as Blacks, or $43,800 versus $3,700. The median white household controls $6,999 in net financial assets, while the median black household has no net financial assets. Net worth is the sum of all assets less debt. Net financial assets excludes from that figure equity accrued in a home or vehicle.[66]

Community-Based Employment

Phase two in the final step is community-based employment. Historically, our communities have suffered through mixed results in

---

65   Bernard W. Kinsey, KBK Enterprises, quote from *The New York Times*, 1 August 1993.
66   Poverty & Race Research Action Council, November/December 1995, Volume 4: Number 6, pg.1.

creating jobs for ourselves. Every business in the black community does not need to be black-owned to be delivering real value to the community. They must be community based. Community-based means that they hire in the community, the owners live in the community, and/or support community based initiatives (after-school programs and youth athletics).

Sugar Ray Robinson once owned a series of buildings and businesses in Harlem that delivered a range of services to black people. All the businesses failed. With the best intentions, black people in the last century have started businesses without the requisite business training or industry expertise. Additionally, we often partner with friends versus people who can deliver value to our enterprises. Hard work will carry you half the way, but industry knowledge and business acumen are also needed to ensure consistent success over time. This fact has hurt everyone from the Nation of Islam to Richard Pryor.

At the end of slavery, 80 percent of the skilled labor work force was black men and women.[67] If our ancestors had just been allowed to practice their trades for a real wage, we would be significantly better off today. Various unions were almost singularly responsible for excluding Blacks from every major and minor labor/construction opportunity in the U.S. It was a white-males-only club that destroyed the black labor base. But, when white people began to abandon their own organizations, we were happy to pay those union dues and keep the various unions afloat.

The greatest creator of black business in America during the 1960s were the urban riots. This turmoil was partially responsible for millions of dollars flowing to groups of black people. The number of high profile black businesses created during this time is staggering. Essence Communications, Black Enterprise, UniWorld Group, Burrell Advertising, Soul Train, and Tony Brown's Journal to name just a few. The founders of these organizations are to be commended for successfully navigating these businesses toward the 21st Century. Equally striking is the number of black power brokers who came out of this period. Colin Powell, Vernon Jordan, Marion Berry, Andrew Young, Thomas Sowell, Willie Brown, and Clarence Thomas were all touched by white mentors during the late 60s and early 70s.

---

67 Quote from Dr. Tony Martin at the First World Lecture Series, Harlem, New York, 1 March 1997.

Today, we can not count on dollars flowing into our communities to start businesses. We must launch businesses through the pooling of resources and talent, as many other groups have successfully done.

Business Creation

The final phase of the model is business creation. Playing the lottery is not a vehicle for creating economic development. It is the action of a desperate people who have given up on their own ability to create a better life. In 1997, one predominately African-American ward in Chicago spent $70 million in lottery tickets.[68] In my experience no single ethnic or racial group in America has come up with more good ideas than African American people. Unfortunately, we are also the people who have implemented the fewest ideas. Two overlooked but prominent weaknesses in most business plans are strategic thinking and investment-friendly analytics. Business plans that are strong in both these areas are more likely to attract investments. Today, there is more investment capital looking for good investments than there are good investments.

Strategic thinking begins with the three Cs: customers, company, and competition. Who is your customer? What do they want from your product or service? Why do they want it? When do they want it? These are simple questions. In their simplicity, they demand that you answer them with data and information from focus groups (structured conversations with prospective customers), surveys, and competitive intelligence (detailed research on competition), not just intuition and guess work. A business plan must be firmly grounded in a fundamental understanding of the target consumer. Company analysis requires you to understand your organization's strengths and weaknesses, as well as any unique opportunities or threats that exist in the marketplace. Competitive analysis is an area of major weakness in many business plans. Some entrepreneurs make the mistake of believing they are smarter and more resourceful than their competition. As a principle, it is always better to not underestimate your competition. Similar to company analysis, competitive analysis requires you to understand your competition's strengths and weaknesses, as well as any unique opportunities or threats that exist for them. In addition, you must invest time in competitive scenario analysis.

---

68 *The St. Louis American*, Jesse Jackson, 6-12 August 1998, pg. A3.

If you do x, will your competitor do a, b, or c? The more you know about your competition, the better you will be able to predict their activities.

As an investor, I want to know what your business can provide me as an investment vehicle. A quality business plan must clearly define in a financial sense what the investors get and when they will get it. It is not within the scope of this book to define all the necessary financial elements to a quality business plan, but there are several key principles. First, return on investment (ROI) is a critical measure. It depends on the industry, but an investor will expect the ROI on your business to be at least 20 percent over the life of their investment. Second, offer the investor only the relevant numbers. Do not fill a business plan with useless financial numbers and charts. You must know what the critical financial numbers are for your business and your industry. Third, search for every tax benefit available. Based on the structure of your organization and the products/services offered, you could be missing out on major tax savings or benefits. Your competitors will not make the same mistake.

Anything of value takes effort to achieve. The greater the value, the greater the effort required to achieve it. Creating a business is hard work. As African American entrepreneurs, we must work together if we are to build the organizations that our communities so desperately need. Strategic thinking and investor-focused financials will get you one step closer to creating a successful business.

It is important to reflect on past entrepreneurial successes of black inventors. As a group, African Americans were responsible for as many as 1,000 patents by 1913. Inventions included automatic lubrication for stream engines, the first machine for mass-producing shoes, the first automatic stoplight, and 35 patents for various electromechanical devices. Unfortunately, these entrepreneurs and scientists rarely benefited financially from their creations.

African Americans were responsible for $460 billion in consumer spending in 1996. The opportunities to create wealth are greater than ever. Advanced technologies are beginning to level the playing field for entrepreneurs. As we enter the 21st Century, our economic development agenda must include the complete ownership of our creativity. The easiest thing to control is that which you produce.

Additional Resources

Books

Porter, Michael (1980) *Competitive Strategy.* New York: The Free Press.

Porter, Michael (1985) *Competitive Advantage.* New York: The Free Press.

Brandenburger, Adam and Nalebuff, Barry (1996) *Co-opetition.* New York: Currency Doubleday.

Ohmae, Kenichi (1982) *The Mind of the Strategist.* New York: McGraw Hill, Inc.

McKenna, Regis (1997) *Real Time.* Boston: Harvard Business School Press.

Lewis, Reginal and Walker, Blair (1995) *Why Should White Guys Have All The Fun?* New York, John Wiley & Sons, Inc.

World Wide Web

Jim Brown (http://pathfinder.com/photo/essay/african/cap10.htm)

The Charlie Rose Show (www.pbs.org/charlierose)

Sugar Ray Robinson (www.worldboxing.com/classics/sugarray.htm)

Harlem (www.hometoharlem.com)

The American Civil War (www.cwc.lsu.edu)

Essence Communications (www.essence.com)

Black Enterprise (www.blackenterprise.com)

Tony Brown's Journal (www.tonybrown.com)

Mayor Willie Brown (www.ci.sf.ca.us/mayor/index.htm)

U.S. Small Business Administration (www.sba.gov)

Organizations

American Association of Black Women Entrepreneurs
P.O. Box 13933
Silver Springs, MD 20911-3933
301.565.0258

Center for Entrepreneurial Management
180 Varick Street, Penthouse
New York, NY 10014
212.633.0060

Center for Family Business
P.O. Box 24268
Cleveland, OH 44124
216.442.0800

Minority Business Development Agency
U.S. Department of Commerce
Washington, DC 20230
(check *Yellow Pages* for local chapters)

STEP FIVE

National Association of Negro Business & Professional Women
    1806 New Hampshire Avenue, NW
    Washington, DC 20009
    202.483.4206
Small Business Administration
    1110 Vermont Avenue, NW
    Washington, DC 20005
    202.606.4000
    (check *Yellow Pages* for your local office)
Washington Interdependence Council
    2020 Pennsylvania Avenue, N.W., Suite 225
    Washington, DC 20006
    202.387.3380; 202.387.6976
    Merging Civic and Market Interests for a Better Tomorrow

TWENTY KEYS TO A SUCCESSFUL
& HAPPY LIFE

1. Value every woman you see as if she was your mother.
2. Surround yourself with people that you want to be like.
3. Take responsibility for everything you do, the good and the bad.
4. Replace the words nigger, bitch, and motherfucker with brother, sister, and friend.
5. Transition from intimidation and violence to quiet confidence and discipline.
6. Spend more time reading books than watching television.
7. Buy more books than music CDs.
8. Read all five of Dr. Cheikh Anta Diop's books.
9. Help people who want to help themselves.
10. Invest your money in your community.
11. Support organizations and institutions that value your existence.
12. Worship a God that looks like you.
13. Practice a religion that views women as the equal of men.
14. Start a family only after you are twenty-five years old.
15. Always ask why, accept few things as fact.
16. Set high goals and create a detailed plan to achieve them.
17. Get as many educational degrees as you can afford as early as possible in your life.
18. Drink at least eight glasses of water per day.
19. Eat as many uncooked, unprocessed food as possible.
20. Pick up one piece of litter every day.

HISTORY TIMELINE

Date	Event
2.5 mm.	Homo habilis (African) appears
1.0 mm.	Homo erectus (African) appears
150000	Homo sabiens sapiens (African) appears
43000	Africans begin iron mining in the Nile Valley
33000	Invasion of Europe by the Grimaldi Negroid from Africa
30000	Africans of Monomotapa create the first sculpture of a human figure
30000	Arrival of Australians in Australia
20000	First Cro-Magnon in Europe
17850	Africans cultivating and harvesting barley and einkorn wheat in the Nile Valley
15000	Africans in Kenya domesticate cattle
12000	Sebelian II rules in Pre-Dynastic Kemet
10000	The first calendar is introduced by the Africans of the Nile Valley
8000	Sebelian III rules in Pre-Dynastic Kemet
6020	Africans in the Congo use markings on bones to develop a numeration system
4100	The first solar calendar is introduced by Kemet and Kush
3800	Emergence of earliest Nubian civilization
3758	The world's first religious principles are written by the Kushite, King Ori
3400	Nubian Kingdom of Ta-Seti founded
3150	King Narmer unifies Upper and Lower Kemet, establishes Memphis as capital

3000	Modern West Africans develop more complex societies in Nigeria
2980	King Khasekhemuwy rules in Kemet during the 2nd Dynasty
2900	Kush invades and establishes the Kingdom of Elam in the Empire of Persia
2685	The Grand Lodge of Luxor was built at Danderah by Khufu
2650	Imhotep of builds Step Pyramid and Saqqara complex during Zoser's reign
2500	Indus Valley civilization in India, Dravidians from Africa are foundation builders
2465	All great pyramids at Dahshur and Giza, temples and mortuary complexes completed
2323	Pyramid Texts inscribed in tomb of King Unas
2300	An African King rules Mesopotamia, King Patesi (Gudea)of Lagash
2150	Kemet experiences cultural upheaval (until 2040 B.C.E.)
2040	Mentuhotep II unifies Kemet and relocates the capital to Waset
2000	Beginning of the Kingdom of Cush in Sudan with its capital at Kerma
1897	Amenemhet constructs the great Kemetic Labyrinth
1783	First Asian invasion of Kemet by Hyksos (until 1550 B.C.E.)
1700	Agricultural revolution in sub-Saharan Africa
1550	King Ahmose defeats the Hyksos and reunifies Kemet
1504	Thutmose I expands rulership to include Persia and Iraq
1500	Beginning of the Olmecs in Mexico (to 800 B.C.E.)
1473	Queen Hatshepsut rules Kemet as first female pharaoh
1391	Thutmose III rules Kemet, great military power, Queen Tiye rules by his side
1353	Amenhotep IV introduces concepts of Aton as the only God in Kemet
1333	Tutankhamen become the king
1306	Seti I, the father of Rameses II, builds major tomb in the Valley of the Kings

1290	Rameses II (Rameses the Great) rules Kemet for 67 years
1070	Period of great social, political, and religious decline in Kemet (until 750 B.C.E.)
970	Cush becomes an independent kingdom with the capital at Napata on the Nile
760	King Kashta rules Meroe until 751
751	Piye (Piankhi), Nubian king, conquers Upper and Lower Kemet removing foreigners
716	King Shabato rules Meroe until 701
690	Taharqa leads military invasion of Spain and Palestine
667	Nubians battle Assyrians for both Lower and Upper Kemet
600	Pharaoh Necho (Niku) II commissions Hanno to circumnavigate Africa
548	The Secret Temple of the Mysteries System of Delfi is burnt to the ground
538	King Analma'aye rules Kush until 533
533	King Amani-natake-lebte rules Kush until 513
525	Kemet invaded by Cambyses and becomes a part of the Persian Empire
513	King Korkamani rules Kush until 503
503	King Amani-astabarqa rules Kush until 478
500	Nok culture thrives in western Sudan (Nigeria)
478	King Sisaspiqa rules Kush until 458
460	Herodotus arrives in Kemet searching for knowledge
458	King Nasakhma rules Kush until 453
453	King Malewiebamani rules Kush until 423
423	King Talakhamani rules Kush until 418
418	King Aman-nete-yerike rules Kush until 398
398	King Baskakeren rules Kush until 397
397	King Harisiotet rules Kush until 362
380	30th Dynasty is last period of rulership by native-born Kemetic (ends 343 B.C.E.)
342	King Akhratan rules Kush until 328
332	Alexander the Great defeats the Persian army and conquers Kemet

CULTURAL & ECONOMIC REVITALIZATION

328	King Nastasen rules Kush until 308
300	In Kush, royal institution of the Kentake (Candaces), or Queen Mother, is established
300	Africans in Kenya develop a calendar system based on astronomical reckoning
280	Merotic Script, an indigenous form of written communication is introduced
260	Queen Bartare rules Meroe until 250
250	Zenith of Meroitic civilization until 100 A.D.
218	Hannibal leads his army across the Alps to challenge Rome
170	Queen Shanakdakhete rules Meroe until 160
41	Queen Amanishabhete rules Meroe until 12; Roman invasion occurs in 23
30	Augustus Caesar claims Egypt as a province of Rome
22	Africans living in Tanzania produce carbon steel in 1,800° C blast furnaces
12	Queen Amaritare rules Meroe until 12 A.D.
62	Queen Amanikhastashan rules Meroe (Nubia) until 85 C.E.
100	Hausa Bokwoi rose as an empire in Nigeria (beginning as separate states)
300	States of Takrur and Ghana founded
330	Conquest of Meroitic Empire by Nuba; Aksum becomes commercial center
350	Aksumite king Ezana converts to Christianity and declares it the state religion
391	Christian Emperor Theodosius bans the ancient religious systems of Egypt
527	Christian Emperor Justinian closes the last Egyptian temple at Philae
550	Emperor Kanissa-ai of Ghana chooses Koranga as his capital; mother's birthplace
641	Moslems first invasion of Nubia (Sudan)
642	Conquest of Egypt by Arabs and the introduction of Islam
700	States of Gao and Kanem founded (until 900)

715	The first Moorish Dynasty, the Umayyad, ruled Spain from 715 to 750
846	Founding of the Kanem-Bornu kingdom east of Lake Chad
880	The Yoruba founded Ife, still the spiritual centre of Yorubaland
900	Kingdom of Ghana
990	Grasslanders move into the forests of Nigeria, begin dynasties at Oyo and Benin
1000	Islam moves into sub-Saharan Africa
1000	Great Zimbabwe is the capital of Mwenetupa Empire in Southern Africa
1050	Mandingo king Baramendana Keita converts to Islam by his own choosing
1054	Muslim Berbers (Almoravids) declare a jihad against the Kingdom of Ghana
1067	Tunka Menin rules the Empire of Ghana
1087	Kanem-Bornu converts to Islam
1100	Kingdom of Benin (until 1897)
1116	According to Idrisi, the emperor of Ghana lived in a castle with glass windows
1200	Establishment of Hausa kingdoms in west Africa; first kingdom: Daura
1203	Fall of the kingdom of Ghana to the Sosso
1230	The fourth and last Moorish Dynasty, the Almohade falls in Spain
1230	Kingdom of Mali established under King Sundiata Keita (ruled 1230-1255)
1290	Dogon of Mali plot the orbits of various star systems, including Sirius B1
1300	The slave trade greatly expands in northern Africa, Ethiopia, and West Africa
1324	Emperor of Mali, Mansa Mussa goes to Mecca with an entourage of 60,000
1332	Death of Mansa Mussa, the great king of Mali (ruled 1307-1332)

1375	Gao secedes from Mali, eventually becomes the Songhai Empire
1415	Portuguese battle Arabs and Moors in Ceuta in Morocco
1420	Minority Tutsi follow Hutu into Rwanda and establish a feudal monarchy
1438	The Portuguese travel down the coast of Africa
1440	Eware the Great (ruled 1440-1473) expands Benin into a great forest empire
1442	The Portuguese buy a few African prisoners of war from other Africans
1450	Decline of the Kingdom of Mali; rise of the Songhai Empire
1460	Cayor emancipates itself from Mali to become an independent province
1465	Seven Cayorian dynasties last until 1870; they never embraced Islam
1468	Sonni Ali conquers Timbuktu, removing the Tuaregs who cause much damage
1484	The Fung Kingdom reigns in Sudan until 1790
1493	Muhammad Touré (1493-1528) assumes power in Songhai; it becomes Muslim
1500	Consolidation of Songhai Empire under Askia Muhammed
1517	Egypt conquered by the Turks of the Ottoman Empire
1518	The first enslaved Africans arrived in North and South America, and the Caribbean
1529	Muslim state of Adal declares a jihad against Christian Ethiopia, conquers
1538	The first recorded importation of Africans into Brazil
1541	Ethiopia defeat of the Muslims
1549	The zenith of the Songhai Empire under Askia Daud (1549-1582)
1569	The Great Mosque of Timbuktu is restored by Cadi El Aquib
1593	Moroccans defeat the Songahai with the help of firearms; rape of men and women

HISTORY TIMELINE

1593	University of Sankoré, in Timbuktu, is destroyed by Arabs and the faculty is exiled
1593	The Sudanese scholar Ahmed Baba loses 1,600 books during forced exile by Arabs
1596	Askia Nuh does not accept Arab domination and organizes national resistance in West Africa
1606	Enslaved Africans in Brazil establish a Maroon settlement known as Palmares
1623	Queen Nzingha becomes Monarch of Ndanga and declares war on Portuguese
1655	1,500 enslaved Africans go to Jamaican mountains, establishing free Maroon towns
1663	Slave rebellion takes place on September 13th in Gloucester County, Virginia
1672	Charles the II of England charters the Royal African Company for slave trading
1695	King Zumbi of Palmares is killed by the Portuguese; Palmares is destroyed (November 20th)
1712	A slave insurrection occurred April 7th in New York City
1739	The Maroons of Jamaica and the British sign a peace treaty on March 1st
1739	Led by Cato on September 9th, slaves rebel and kill more than 25 enslavers
1753	Benjamin Banneker builds the first All-American clock with wood
1770	Crispus Attucks is one of the first to die for America at the Boston Massacre (March 5th)
1772	Lord Mansfield declares exportation of slaves from Britain illegal
1772	James Somerset becomes *de facto* spokesman for Blacks in Britain
1773	*Poems on Various Subjects, Religious and Moral* was published by Phillis Wheatley
1774	Henry Smeathmen proposes to British government to set up a colony in Sierra Leone
1776	During American Revolution, many Blacks fight for British promised freedom

69

1777	The Republic of Vermont passes the first constitution in the U.S. prohibiting slavery
1777	5,000 Africans participate in the U.S. Revolutionary War
1783	Blacks establish settlements in Nova Scotia separately from Whites; not recognized
1786	Quakers in Pennsylvania begin to organize the Underground Railroad
1786	Blacks in London sign up for colony at Sierra Leone; disembark from ship in February 1787
1787	King Naimbana of Temnes permits colony to settle in treaty with British
1787	Free African Society is founded in Philadelphia by Richard Allen and Absalom Jones
1790	Sierra Leone disastrous failure, most die from disease; town is destroyed by locals
1790	Discontented Blacks arrive from Nova Scotia and are met by Granville Town survivors
1791	Benjamin Banneker plays critical role in surveying and designing Washington, DC
1791	Benjamin Banneker publishes his first Almanac
1793	Congress passes the first Fugitive Slave Act on February 12th
1794	Sierra Leone attacked by French privateers; colony liberated in two months
1795	Jean Baptist Pointe DuSable establishes a trading post at mouth of Chicago River
1798	Egypt conquered by Napoleon of France
1801	Africans led by Toussaint L'Ouverture revolt and seize power in Haiti from France
1801	War in Sierre Leone (ends 1807)
1803	Sierra Leone Co. petitions British Parliament for loans; rejected over four years
1806	Benjamin Banneker dies (October 9th)
1807	Colony comes under rule directly from London, and Sierra Leone Co. is dissolved
1807	The British Parliament bans the slave trade

HISTORY TIMELINE

1808	The importation of enslaved Africans is forbidden by the U.S.; law is ignored
1810	The Afro-American Insurance Company is established by three black men
1811	Paul Cuffe, a Black, begins transporting Blacks from North America back to Africa
1815	Fulani Emirs declared a jihad against the Hausa state of Gobir
1818	Frederick Douglass is born on Maryland's Eastern Shore in February
1820	Mohammad Ali of Egypt captures Sudan
1822	African Americans settlers found Monrovia, capital of Liberia
1822	George Wilson, a Black, tells white slavers of Denmark Vesey's plan to lead a major revolt
1823	Alexander Lucius Twilight graduates from Middlebury College
1827	The first African American newspaper is published, *Freedom's Journal*
1831	The Honorable Nat Turner begins his fight for freedom in Virginia, 60 slavers killed
1832	The anti-slavery Abolitionist Party is founded in Boston
1833	Enslaved people are freed in all British possessions
1834	Henry Blair is first African American to be granted a U.S. patent, for a seed planter
1837	Aleksandr Sergeyevich Pushkin, Russian of African descent, is killed in duel
1838	The first African American magazine is published, *The Mirror of Liberty*
1839	Frederick Douglass escapes from slavery
1839	Slaves revolt on Spanish ship *Amistad* and secure freedom via Supreme Court
1841	William Liedesdorff from Virgin Islands becomes first African American millionaire
1843	U.S. Patent Office issues Norbert Rillieux patent for a system of refining sugar
1844	Macon B. Allen is admitted to the bar in Maine to practice law as a licensed attorney

1845	Autobiography *Narrative of the Life of Frederick Douglass* is published
1847	Liberia becomes an independent republic on July 26th
1847	Frederick Douglass begins publishing *The North Star*, an anti-slavery journal
1849	Harriet Tubman escapes from slavery; returns to South over 20 times to free others
1850	Slave trade is forbidden in the District of Columbia
1850	Emperor Tewodros II led campaigns against Egyptian intruders
1852	Martin R. Delany publishes *The Condition, Elevation, Emigration, and Destiny...*
1853	William Wells Brown's novel *The President's Daughter* is published
1854	The first modern college for Blacks established, Ashmun Institute (Lincoln University)
1855	Founder of modern Ethiopia, Emperor Tewodros II, unifies nation, teaches Menelik
1857	The Supreme Court denies Blacks U.S. citizenship; Dred Scott loses his case
1859	Militantly anti-slavery, John Brown is hung for treason after raiding a federal arsenal
1859	Harriet Wilson's novel *Our Nig* is published
1860	Isaac Myers begins organizing the Colored National Labor Union
1861	Yoruba, attacked by black Muslims, draws closer to Britain, which annexes Lagos
1862	Ida B. Wells is born on July 16th
1862	186,000 Africans serve during the Civil War; 38,000 die in service
1863	The first school for freed enslaved people is founded in Frogmore, South Carolina
1863	Abraham Lincoln issues the Emancipation Proclamation
1863	William Brown publishes *The Black Man: His Antecedents, His Genius, and His Achievements*
1864	The Ku Klux Klan is organized in Pulaski, Tennessee

1864	During the Berlin Conference of 1884-85, European countries plot the near complete colonization of Africa
1865	General Lee surrenders to General Grant at Appomattox ending the U.S. Civil War
1865	The Thirteenth Amendment, which outlaws slavery in the U.S., is ratified
1866	Fisk University is established in Knoxville, Tennessee
1867	Negro League Baseball begins in early spring until late fall, then the Winter season
1867	Sarah Breedlove (Madam C.J. Walker) is born on a Mississippi River plantation in Delta, LA to former enslaved people, Owens and Minerva Breedlove
1868	The Fourteenth Amendment, validating citizenship rights for all persons born in the U.S.
1869	British and other Ethiopians encircle Emperor Tewrodos II; he commits suicide
1870	The ratification of Fifteenth Amendment secures voting rights for all male U.S. citizens
1870	A European, Thomas M. Peterson is the first African American to vote
1874	Blanche Kelso Bruce becomes the first African American senator to serve a full term
1876	Edward Alexander Bouchet receives a Ph.D. in physics from Yale University
1879	The Zulus defeat the British for the last time in The Battle of Isandlwana
1879	A European, Dr. Felkin witnesses a caesarean operation by Banyoro surgeons in Uganda
1881	British and Ottoman troops seize control of Egypt and Sudan
1881	Booker T. Washington opens the Tuskegee Institute, an industrial school for Blacks
1883	Spelman College is founded in Atlanta, Georgia
1884	Granville T. Woods secures his first patent in 1884 for a steam boiler furnace
1884	British control of Nigeria expanded, set up under treaties with Yoruba rulers

1885	Mohammed-Ahmed, a Sudanese defeats Anglo-Arab army recapturing much land
1885	Belgium colonizes Zaire as Congo Free State
1885	A patent is awarded to Sarah Goode for a folding cabinet bed
1886	Menelik moves the Ethiopian capital to the Intoto Valley (Addis Ababa)
1886	Frederick Douglass travels to Africa and climbs one of the pyramids
1887	Ethiopians defeat a small contingent of Italians near Dogali
1887	The Honorable Marcus Garvey is born in Jamaica, August 17th (St. Ann's Bay)
1887	Granville T. Woods patents the rail telegraph system
1889	Ida B. Wells becomes editor of the Free Press and the Highlight
1889	Menelik II is crowned the new Emperor and he makes a treaty with Italy
1891	Provident Hospital in Chicago, Illinois becomes the first African American Hospital
1892	Ida B. Wells is the first writer to document the lynching of African Americans
1892	Sarah Boone receives a patent for an ironing board
1895	Paul Laurence Dunbar's poetry collection *Majors and Minors* is published
1895	Frederick Douglass dies
1896	Near Adwa, Ethiopia defeats the Italian colonial army and kills 12,000
1896	Paul Laurence Dunbar's poetry collection *Lyrics of Lowly Life* is published
1896	U.S. Supreme Court says that *separate but equal* does not violate the Constitution
1898	Paul Robeson is born in New Jersey on April 9th, son of an escaped enslaved person
1899	Dr. George F. Grant patented the wooden golf tee (Patent #638,920)
1900	Britain controls Nigeria

HISTORY TIMELINE

1900	The first Pan-African Congress convenes in London
1901	James and J. Rosamond Johnson write "Lift Every Voice and Sing"
1901	Booker T. Washington's autobiography *Up from Slavery* is published
1903	DuBois's collection *The Souls of Black Folks: Essays and Sketches* is published
1903	Future Heavyweight Champ Jack Johnson plays first base for the Philadelphia Giants
1903	Maggie Lena Walker becomes Bank President of St. Luke Bank and Trust Company
1903	Williams and Walker open "In Dahomey," the first all black musical on Broadway
1904	Madam C.J. Walker works as an agent for Annie (Pope Tumbo) Malone, founder of the Pore Company, an early manufacturer of hair care products for black women
1904	The Atlanta debate between W.E.B. DuBois and Booker T. Washington occurs
1904	Philip Payton founds the Afro-American Realty Company in New York City
1905	The Niagara Movement is established; among its leaders is W.E.B. DuBois
1905	In Negro Baseball League, good teams in major cities make money, white league does not
1905	Madam C.J. Walker moves to Denver where she establishes her own hair care products company
1907	Alain Locke is the first African American Rhodes Scholar
1908	Jack Johnson wins the World Heavyweight Boxing Championship
1909	The NAACP is founded in New York; almost all the signers of the charter are white
1909	Kwame Nkrumah is born on September 18th in the village of Nkroful, Ghana
1909	Matthew Henson reaches the North Pole
1910	The Hilldale Club of Negro Baseball and their stadium is owned by a black man
1910	Madame C.J. Walker establishes a manufacturing plant in Indianapolis

1910	Granville T. Woods, master inventor (over 60 patents in his name), dies
1911	National Urban League is founded in New York City
1911	Madam C.J. Walker pledges $1,000 to the building fund of Indianapolis's new black YMCA
1912	W. C. Handy published the first blues song, "Memphis Blues" on September 27th
1912	James Weldon Johnson's *The Autobiography of an Ex-Coloured Man* is published
1913	Menelik II dies and is succeeded by his grandson Lej Isayu
1914	The Universal Negro Improvement and Conservation Association and African Communities League is launched by the Honorable Marcus Garvey
1914	Nigerian Council is established with six African and 30 European set up to advise governor
1915	The great migration of southern Blacks to the North begins; industry needs labor
1916	Belgium takes over rule of Burundi and Rwanda
1916	350,000 African Americans serve during World War I
1917	Race riots in East St. Louis, Illinois
1917	Silent Protest Parade in New York City on July 27th
1918	The Honorable Marcus Garvey incorporates the UNIA in the U.S.
1918	Manuel R. Querino publishes *The African Contribution to Brazilian Civilization*
1918	The French award the Croix de Guerre to the 369th Regiment (WWI) and named it "Harlem Hell Fighters"
1919	Oscar Micheaux finishes his first film, *The Homesteader*
1919	Paul Robeson graduates Valedictorian, Phi Beta Kappa, All-American from Rutgers
1919	Madam C.J. Walker hosts a meeting of the International League of Darker People with Marcus Garvey
1919	W.E.B. DuBois organizes the first Pan-African Congress in Paris
1921	Bessie Coleman earns an international pilot's license
1921	Henry Pace forms the Pace Phonographic Corporation, owns the Black Swan label

HISTORY TIMELINE

1922	Legislative Council (ten Africans [four elected] and 36 Europeans) in Nigeria
1922	Jack Johnson, former Boxing Champ, patents a theft-prevention device for vehicles
1922	Claude McKay's poetry collection *Harlem Shadows* is published
1923	Harlem Renaissance Basketball Club founded
1923	Ethiopia becomes a member of the League of Nations
1923	Garrett A. Morgan receives a patent for the first automatic traffic light
1923	Paul Robeson graduates from Columbia Law School
1923	Marcus Garvey's *The Philosophy & Opinion of Marcus Garvey* is published
1923	Jean Toomer's prose collection *Cane* is published
1924	Paul Robeson stars in *The Emperor Jones* in the Provincetown Theatre
1924	Paul Robeson stars in his first film, *Body and Soul,* by Oscar Micheaux
1925	The Division of Negro Literature, History, and Prints (Schomburg Center) opens
1925	*The New Negro: An Interpretation* is published, recognizing Harlem Renaissance
1925	The Honorable Marcus Garvey is betrayed by his own people and is sent to prison
1926	Carter G. Woodson creates Negro History Week
1927	Langston Hughes's poetry collection *Fine Clothes to the Jew* is published
1927	James W. Johnson's *God's Trombones: Seven Negro Sermons in Verse* is published
1929	Dr. Martin Luther King, Jr. was born on January 15, 1929, in Atlanta, Georgia
1929	The U.S. stock market crash sends Madam C.J. Walker Manufacturing Company into a financial crisis.
1930	Ras Tafari Mekonen crowned Emperor Haile Selasie after death of Empress
1930	The first Temple of Islam is founded in Detroit, Michigan

1930	The Kansas City Monarchs have the first portable light system in Negro Baseball
1930	Paul Robeson stars in the London production of Shakespeare's *Othello*
1931	Ida B. Wells joins her ancestors on March 25th
1933	H. Naylor Fitzhugh is one of the first African American graduates of Harvard Business School
1933	The publication of journal *Létudiant Noir* marks birth of negritude movement
1934	Paul and Essie Robeson travel to Soviet Union at invitation of Russian film director
1935	Negro Baseball League is stable; biggest black business, $2 million per year
1935	Mary McLeod Bethune founds the National Council of Negro Women
1935	Harlem Race Riot occurs
1935	Kwame Nkrumah is introduced to *The Philosophy & Opinions of Marcus Garvey*
1936	Jesse Owens wins four gold medals at the Olympics in Berlin, Germany
1936	Josh Gibson, a catcher for the Negro League's Pittsburgh Crawfords, hits 84 home runs in one season
1937	Zora Neale Hurston's novel *Their Eyes Were Watching God* is published
1937	W.E.B. DuBois and Paul Robeson are co-founders of Council on African Affairs
1939	Aimé F. Césaire, Father of Negritude, uses word in *Cahier d'un retour au pays natal*
1940	The Honorable Marcus Garvey dies with a broken heart on June 10th
1940	American Negro Theatre founded
1940	Richard Wright publishes the novel *Native Son*
1942	John H. Johnson publishes *Negro Digest* in November with a $500 loan
1943	Poor people in Ethiopia revolt in Tigray
1943	With Paul Robeson, *Othello* breaks Broadway records

1944	The U.S. Supreme Court rules that no American can be denied the right to vote
1944	The United Negro College Fund is founded on April 24th
1945	Dr. Lloyd A. Quarterman receives award of appreciation for Atomic Bomb work
1945	John Coltrane has his first professional jazz appearance, playing alto sax with the Jimmy Johnson Big Band
1945	The Negro Leagues reach a plateau of stability and efficiency
1945	Gwendolyn Brooks's poetry collection *A Street in Bronzeville* is published
1945	Richard Wright's *Black Boy: A Record of Childhood and Youth* is published
1946	Takala Walda-Hawaryat opposes the return of exiled Emperor Selasie; is detained
1946	Jackie Robinson integrates into the White Baseball League
1946	*The Street*, published by Ann Petry, sells more than one million copies
1947	Every team in the Negro Leagues loses money; fans more interested in integration and white baseball
1947	*Présence Africaine*, a literary journal is founded by Senghor, Césaire, and Demas
1947	John Hope Franklin publishes *From Slavery to Freedom*
1947	John Coltrane has a jam session with Charlie Parker
1947	The new Nigeria Council had 28 African (four elected) and 17 European members
1948	Apartheid is instituted in South Africa; it calls for the supremacy of Whites
1948	U.S. President Harry Truman bans segregation in the armed forces
1949	Singer Juanita Hall is the first African American to receive a Tony award
1950	The U.S. government takes Paul Robeson's passport and attempts to silence him
1950	Kwame Nkrumah is arrested and imprisoned by the British
1950	Ralph Bunche receives the Nobel Peace Prize for his work as a mediator in Palestine

1950	John Coltrane (on alto sax) has a recording session with Dizzy Gillespie and his orchestra
1950	Gwendolyn Brooks is awarded a Pulitzer Prize for *Annie Allen*
1952	Africans rebel against British rule in the Mau-Mau uprisings in Kenya (until 1956)
1952	On March 5th, Kwame Nkrumah is named the Prime Minister of Ghana
1952	John Coltrane plays with Miles Davis and Sonny Rollins at the Audubon Ballroom in Harlem
1953	James Baldwin publishes *Go Tell It on the Mountain*
1953	Ralph Ellison receives the National Book Award for fiction for *Invisible Man*
1954	A further constitution declares Nigeria a federation
1954	U.S. Supreme Court rules that racial segregation in public schools is unconstitutional
1954	George and Joan Johnson found the Johnson Product Company
1955	Dr. Cheikh Anta Diop publishes *Nations Nègres et Culture*
1955	Rosa Parks refuses to give up her seat to white man on a Montgomery, Alabama bus
1956	U.S. Supreme Court outlaws segregated seating on buses
1956	The First Congress of African Writers is held in Paris
1957	John Coltrane experiences his spiritual rebirth, no more drugs
1957	The Southern Christian Leadership Conference is formed on February 14th
1957	Kwame Nkrumah leads Ghana to independence on March 5th
1957	U.S. Congress passes the Voting Rights Act of 1957
1957	Internal self-government was gained by the Eastern and Western regions of Nigeria
1957	*Black Orpheus*, a journal of African writing is established in Nigeria
1958	The U.S. government returns Paul Robeson's passport, his health is poor

1958	Addis Ababa became the registered office for the Economic Commission for Africa
1958	*The Book of Negro Folklore*, edited by Arna Bontemps and Langston Hughes is published
1958	Chinua Achebe's novel *Things Fall Apart* is published
1958	Paul Robeson's autobiography *Here I Stand* is published
1959	Internal self-government is gained by Northern Nigeria
1959	Berry Gordy establishes Motown Records in Detroit, Michigan
1959	Lorraine Hansberry's play *A Raisin in the Sun* is produced and published
1959	Ruth Bowen establishes the Queen Booking Company, a talent agency in NYC
1960	Nigeria is free
1960	Ghana is declared a republic and Nkrumah becomes its first President on July 1st
1960	Congo becomes an independent nation
1960	South African police fire on demonstrators at Sharpeville; murdering 67
1960	Marion Barry founds the Student Nonviolent Coordinating Committee (SNCC)
1960	Poor people in Ethiopia revolt in Sidamo
1960	A coup by General Mengistu Naway and Garwane Naway fails in Ethiopia
1961	Led by Julius Nyerere, Tanganyika achieves independence from Britain
1961	A. Phillip Randolph's march in Washington D.C.
1961	Wilt Chamberlain scores 100 points in a single basketball game
1961	Bob Marley, Bunny Livingston, and Peter Tosh form a group called the Rudeboys
1961	Ossie Davis's play *Purlie Victorious* is produced and published
1962	Rwanda and Burundi gain independence
1962	John Coltrane has a recording session with Duke Ellington

1963	Under the leadership of Jomo Kenyatta, Kenya achieves independence from Britain
1963	Frantz Fanon publishes *The Wretched of the Earth*
1963	Poor people in Ethiopia revolt in Bale (until 1970)
1963	Medgar Evers is murdered by Klansman in Mississippi June 12th
1963	Nigeria became a Republic with Dr. Nnamdi Azikiwe its first President (October 1st)
1963	A black church is bombed in Birmingham, Alabama killing four girls (September 15th)
1963	W.E.B. DuBois passes away
1963	March on Washington for Jobs and Freedom draws 250,000 demonstrators
1963	The Organization for African Unity is founded in the Ethiopian capital
1963	Queen Mother Moore forms Reparations Committee of Descendants of U.S. Slaves
1963	Gordon Parks's novel *The Learning Tree* is published
1963	Wole Soyinka's plays *The Lion & the Jewel* and *A Dance in the Forest* are published
1964	Al-Hajj Malik Shabazz forms the Organization of Afro-American Unity
1964	John Coltrane records "A Love Supreme," Part I, II, III, and IV
1964	Dr. Martin Luther King, Jr. is awarded the Nobel Prize for Peace
1964	The Civil Rights Act abolishes segregation in public accommodations in the South
1964	Eight African leaders, including Nelson Mandela are sentenced to life in prison
1964	Amiri Baraka's play *Dutchman* is produced and published
1965	Many student demonstrations in the streets of Addis Ababa
1965	Al-Hajj Malik Shabazz is murdered by his own people in front of his family (February 21st at 3:10 P.M.)
1965	*The Autobiography of Malcolm X* is published

1965	Elijah Muhammad publishes *Message to the Blackman in America*
1965	Race riots in the Watts district of L.A.; over $225 million in property damage
1965	A white regime declares Rhodesia independent, civil war begins (until 1979)
1965	The Voting Rights Act provides guarantees for Blacks voting in the South
1966	The first of seven coups in Nigeria occurred in January (many leaders murdered)
1966	While away visiting China, Kwame Nkrumah is overthrown on February 24th
1966	Bobby Seale and Huey Newton found the Black Panther party in Oakland, California
1967	Community Control of Schools Movement initiated at Harlem I.S. 201
1967	John Coltrane opens The Olatumji Center of African Culture in Harlem, New York on March 27th
1967	Eastern Nigeria claims independence as the Republic of Biafra; leads to civil war
1967	John William Coltrane dies in Huntington, Long Island on July 17th
1967	Black Power Conference occurs in Newark, New Jersey
1968	Black Power Conference occurs in Philadelphia, PA
1968	Poor people in Ethiopia revolt in Gojam
1968	Dr. Martin Luther King, Jr. is assassinated in Memphis, Tennessee; riots in 125 cities
1969	Fred Hampton is murdered in Chicago
1969	Black Power Conference in Bermuda, W.I.
1969	U.S. Supreme Court rules that school districts must end racial segregation at once
1969	Toni Morrison's novel *The Bluest Eye* is published
1970	Poor people in Ethiopia revolt in Wolo
1970	Biafra is defeated in January 1970; the war takes one million Nigerian lives
1970	Maya Angelou published *I Know Why the Caged Bird Sings*
1970	Congress of African People occurs in Atlanta, Georgia

CULTURAL & ECONOMIC REVITALIZATION

1971	Ernest J. Gaines's novel *The Autobiography of Miss Jane Pittman* is published
1971	Dr. Yosef A.A. ben-Jochannan publishes *Africa Mother of Western Civilization*
1971	George Jackson murdered on August 21st
1972	Frank Wills, an African American security guard, discovers the Watergate Break-in
1972	Autobiography, *The Man Died: Prison Notes of Wole Soyinka*, is published
1972	On April 27th, Kwame Nhrumah dies in Burcharest
1973	Ayi Kwei Armah publishes *Two Thousand Seasons*
1973	Emperor Haile Selasie is overthrown by a military coup on September 12th
1974	Ethiopian peasants revolt against their feudal exploiters
1975	Arthur Ashe wins the Wimbledon singles title
1975	Emperor Haile Selasie is killed in August and buried under one of his palaces
1975	Another Nigerian coup, new leader Brigadier Murtala Muhammed
1976	Paul Robeson passes on January 23rd
1976	Negro History Week becomes Black History Month
1976	Abortive Nigerian coup, Brigadier Murtala Muhammed is assassinated
1976	Police fire on students and school children in Soweto, South Africa
1976	Alex Haley's novel *Roots: The Saga of an American Family* is published
1976	Ntozake Shange's book *for colored girls who have considered suicide* is produced
1978	National Black Consciousness Day (Zumbi Day) is established in Brazil on November 20th
1978	Muhammad Ali wins the heavyweight boxing championship for a record third time
1978	James A. McPherson receives Pulitzer Prize for short story collection *Elbow Room*
1979	Multi-party elections are held in Nigeria, Alhaji Shehu Shagari becomes President

HISTORY TIMELINE

1980	Freedom fighters destroy Rhodesia; the Republic of Zimbabwe is reestablished
1980	Robert Johnson establishes Black Entertainment Television with a $15,000 loan
1982	Ben Ammi publishes *God, The Black Man and Truth*
1983	Guion S. Bluford, Jr. is the first African American astronaut in space
1983	Gloria Naylor wins an American Book Award for *The Women of Brewster Place*
1983	Alice Walker wins American Book Award and a Pulitzer Prize for *The Color Purple*
1983	President Shagari re-elected in Nigeria
1983	Another Nigerian coup, Major-General Mohammadu Buhari becomes leader
1984	Oprah Winfrey accepts a job as host of "A.M. Chicago," a morning show
1984	Archbishop Desmond Tutu of South Africa receives the Nobel Peace Prize
1984	Amiri Baraka's *The Autobiography of LeRoi Jones* is published
1984	Rev. Jesse Jackson makes a competitive run for U.S. presidency
1985	Another Nigerian coup, new leader Major-General Ibrahim Babangida
1985	Sonia Sanchez receives an American Book Award for *homegirls & handgrenades*
1986	Wole Soyinka is awarded the Nobel Prize for literature
1986	Dr. Cheikh Anta Diop passes on February 7th
1987	Dr. Benjamin Carson is the first to successfully separate Siamese twins joined at head
1987	Ivan Van Sertima publishes *They Came Before Columbus*
1987	Frederick D. Gregory is first person of African ancestry to command a space shuttle
1987	Rita Dove receives a Pulitzer Prize for her poetry collection *Thomas and Beulah*
1987	Dr. Molefi Kete Asante publishes *The Afrocentric Idea*

1987	Reginald Lewis buys Beatrice International Foods for just under $1 billion on August 6th
1988	Terry McMillan wins an American Book Award for her novel *Mama*
1988	Toni Morrison receives a Pulitzer Prize for her novel *Beloved*
1989	Bill White becomes the president of Major League Baseball's National League
1989	Huey P. Newton is murdered by a crack dealer
1989	Ronald H. Brown named Chairman of the Democratic National Committee
1990	F.W. de Klerk pledges to eliminate Apartheid and releases Nelson Mandela
1990	Namibia becomes independent following long struggle to end South African occupation
1990	Charles Johnson receives a National Book Award for his novel *Middle Passage*
1990	August Wilson wins a Pulitzer Prize for his play *The Piano Lesson*
1990	George W. Carver and Percy Julian admitted into National Inventor's Hall of Fame.
1990	L. Douglas Wilder of Virginia becomes the first African American elected governor
1990	"In Living Color" wins an Emmy for Outstanding Comedy Series
1991	Dr. Frances Cress Welsing publishes *The Isis Papers, The Keys to the Colors*
1992	Dr. Mae Jemison travels into space on the space shuttle Endeavor
1992	A race riot sweeps across Los Angeles following the Rodney King verdict
1992	Derek Walcott is awarded the Nobel Prize for literature
1992	Anthony T. Browder publishes *Nile Valley Contributions to Civilization*
1993	Multi-party elections in Nigeria were annulled by Babangida, who after resigned
1993	In Nigeria's seventh modern-age coup, General Sani Abacha assumes power

1993	Toni Morrison wins the Nobel Prize for literature
1993	Arthur Ashe's autobiography *Days of Grace: A Memoir is published*
1994	Llaila O. Afrika publishes *Nutricide: The Nutritional Destruction of the Black Race*
1994	Nelson Mandela takes office as South Africa's first black president
1994	Plane crash kills leaders of both Burundi and Rwanda, unleashing ethnic killing
1995	Over one million men gather in Washington D.C. for the Million Man March
1996	Nigeria wins the Gold Medal in 1996 Olympic Football (Soccer)
1997	Kofi Annan of Ghana becomes the seventh secretary-general of the United Nations
1997	Tiger Woods wins The Masters, breaking several golf records in the process
1997	Laurent Kabila is declared president of the Democratic Republic of Congo
1997	The first made-in-Nigeria saloon car known as Z-600 launched in Owerri
1997	Over one million women gather in Philadelphia for Million Woman March
1997	Multi-party elections begin in Nigeria
1997	Freedom Neruda and Christine Anyanwu win International Press Freedom Prize
1998	Madam C.J. Walker is the subject of a United States Post Office commemorative stamp
1998	Five African nations compete in the Football World Cup
1998	Sani Abacha in Nigeria is poisoned; he is replaced by Abdulsalam Abubakar
1998	Moshood Abiola dies of a heart attack days before his planned release from prison
1998	Thousands of Africans are killed or injured by an Arab bomb attack in Kenya and Tanzania
1999	Al-Hajj Malik Shabazz is the subject of a U.S. Postal Office commemorative stamp
1999	Michael Jordan retires from professional basketball

1999	Nigeria celebrates its new democracy with presidential elections
1999	Venus and Serena Williams win separate professional tennis tournaments on the same day
1999	Nigeria hosts FIFA World Youth Football championship
1999	Nigeria's elected President, General Olusequn Obasanjo, is sworn in on May 29th, ending 15 years of military rule

Note: B.C.E. dates are best approximation

SOURCES FOR TIMELINE

ben-Jochannon, Yosef (1989) *Black Man of the Nile and His Family*. Black Classic Press.

ben-Jochannon, Yosef (1988) *Africa Mother of Western Civilization*. Black Classic Press. Westport, CT: Lawrence Hill Publishers.

Browder, Anthony T. (1992). *Nile Valley Contributions to Civilization*. Washington, D.C.: IKG.

Diop, Cheikh Anta (1974). *The African Origin of Civilization, Myth or Reality*.

Diop, Cheikh Anta (1990). *The Cultural Unity of Black Africa*. Chicago, IL: Third World Press.

Diop, Cheikh Anta (1987). *Precolonial Black Africa*. Westport, CT: Lawrence Hill Publishers.

Diop, Cheikh Anta (1991). *Civilization or Barbarism*. Westport, CT: Lawrence Hill Publishers.

Jackson, John (1990) *Ages of Gold and Silver*. American Atheist Press.Van Sertima, Ivan (1993). *Golden Age of the Moors* (edited by). New Brunswick: Transaction Publishers.

Kush, Indus Khamit (1983). *What They Never Told You in History Class*. New York. D&J Book Distributors.

Obenga, Theophile (1995). *Readings in Precolonial Central Africa*. London: Karnak House.

Williams, Chancellor (1976). *The Destruction of Black Civilization*. Chicago: Third World Press.

ABOUT THE AUTHOR

*M*r. Nique Fajors' summation of experience includes co-founding two companies, launching more than ten consumer and industrial products into various markets, publishing half a dozen articles, developing and producing an acclaimed educational video, *The Invisible Men* and developing an award winning web site, africanhistory.com. Mr. Fajors' work has been profiled in *The Boston Globe, Essence Magazine, The Source,* and *The San Francisco Examiner.*

His professional interests are new media and domestic affairs. Mr. Fajors holds a B.S.B.A. with honors from the Suffolk University Frank Sawyer School of Management and a M.B.A. from the Harvard Business School. He is a member of both *Who's Who Online* and the *International Who's Who of Professionals.* He has traveled and lived in the many of the major cities of North America, Europe, Africa, and Asia. His life credo is discipline, patience, and humility. Mr. Fajors' next book project is a what-if analysis of flashpoints in black history. At present, he is learning to play the jazz trumpet. His e-mail address is nique@cerbook.com

To Place An Order:

- Visit http://www.cerbook.com
- Call 1.800.216.8794
- Fax orders to 1.402.475.1176
- E-mail orders to order@cerbook.com
- Visit your local black-oriented bookstore

Additional Products by Nique Fajors

The Invisible Men, Educational Video ($15.00, 59 minutes, 1995)

*T*he program was created out of a desire to present black youth with a positive view of the future. Sixty minutes in length, consisting of roundtable discussions moderated by Harvard Law School Professor Randall Kennedy, *The Invisible Men* features black men chosen from the Harvard Graduate Schools of Business, Government, and Law. Each contributor is young, accomplished, and goal oriented—the group is representative of the diversity of opinion within the black community.

The "star" of the discussion, however, is an imaginary sixteen-year-old teenager named Darryl, who encounters a series of challenges representative of the problems facing young black males today. The role of the panelists is to assist Darryl while he struggles to survive in a fictitious city called Forgotten, USA. Participants share the lessons they have learned as they debate topics such as education, economic development, and male/female relationships.

For additional information, please send an e-mail message to tim@cerbook.com